His Glory

From Heaven to Earth

KESHAN SINGH

Ark House Press
arkhousepress.com

His Glory
© 2024 KESHAN SINGH

All rights reserved. Apart from any fair dealing for the purpose of study, research, criticism, or review, as permitted under the Copyright Act, no part may be reproduced by any process without written permission.

Scripture taken from the New King James Version®. Copyright © 1982 by Thomas Nelson. Used by permission. All rights reserved.

Cataloguing in Publication Data:
Title: His Glory
ISBN: 978-1-7635572-8-4 (pbk)
Subjects: REL012120 [RELIGION / Christian Living / Spiritual Growth]; REL030000 [RELIGION / Christian Ministry / Evangelism];

Design by initiateagency.com

"For everything comes from God alone.
Everything lives by His power, and everything is for His glory!"

-Romans 11:36

DEDICATION

I want to dedicate this book to every single faithful and obedient servant of Christ our Lord on this Earth.

As each day passes, we are closer to entering into His Kingdom. So, keep pressing on in your walk, remaining faithful to Him, until the Glory of the Father is revealed to us in full measure:

Where we will rest in The Father's arms forever.

Thank you, Helena, I honour you all the days of my life.

Thank you, Andrea, for holding my hand and laying yourself down for me.

"For I consider that the sufferings of this present time are not worthy to be compared with the glory which shall be revealed in us." – Romans 8:18 NKJV

Yes, and Amen.

TABLE OF CONTENTS

Chapter 1
O Lord, My God 1

Chapter 2
Eyes To See and Ears To Hear 17

Chapter 3a
Yod-Heh-Vav-Heh 25

Chapter 3b
Yeshua 70

Chapter 3c
Holy Spirit 95

Chapter 4
The Five-Fold Ministry 105

Chapter 5
The Power of His Word 115

Chapter 6
God's Protection 121

Chapter 7
Salvation Calls 133

FOREWORD

"His Glory" is a unique presentation of the Word of God in a very practical and enjoyable manner.

The author, Keshan Singh has captured the wonders of "His Glory" in this wonderful book which, as he states he wrote with the enabling of the Holy Spirit.

Keshan takes the reader on a journey through the wonders of God in the Old Covenant and meanders into the New Covenant looking at the wonderful work of salvation through our loving Saviour.

He then presents challenges of the "new life" which is enabled by the workings of the third member of the Godhead, the wonderful Holy Spirit.

"His Glory" will leave you in no doubt about the validity of the work of the Cross and presents the reader with opportunities to respond in an affirmative manner.

This book is a must read!

Rev Helena Kauppinen
Senior Minister
Gospel Light Ministries – Upper Room

INTRODUCTION

Our Good Lord Yeshua touched me on the 6th of May, 2023, as I was driving to work, and He told me He wanted me to write a book. He gave me the title for this book – "His Glory". I then saw a vision of a "gold throne, surrounded by clouds", which He revealed to me would be the front cover and the back cover of this book- because He is the beginning and the end.

He gave me the title of the chapters and heavily influenced me by His Spirit, even in this writing of the introduction, to write the content. I pray His love will touch your heart and that His Glory will shine on each page of this book.

For every obedient and faithful servant of our Lord, I speak a blessing of resurrection life into your eyes, that they may be opened to discover His Glory in your life, in all areas, each day.

"I am your shield, your exceedingly great reward." – Genesis 15:1 NKJV

Amen.

CHAPTER 1

O Lord, My God

"Because He has inclined His ear to me, Therefore I will call upon Him as long as I live."- Psalm 116:2 NKJV

When you call out to God, what do you think happens? Do you doubt that any higher power hears you? Do you feel any sensation when you call? Or do you allow your frustration to overflow because you feel there is no immediate response? So much so, to the point that anger takes over and distracts you from the subtle hint or impression in your inner being that someone is in fact, answering you.

You could say that this answering is a "knowing", an "impression", or even just a "feeling". But let me tell you friend, that when the King of all things created (seen and unseen) answers you, you will know it, in your heart of hearts. He will identify Himself to you and you will recognize Him, just like that, without any need for reason or scientific explanation. You may not be able to explain it, but you just know! That is something supernatural, far beyond the minds of humans. This is because all creation, like it or not, will recognize their Creator. Even the animals, insects, trees, waters, winds, planets, all respond when the Good Lord calls.

Unlike us, they actually obey AT FIRST, without question.

Now, why do they obey without question? This is partially because, they have not been given the luxury of a free will, nor the mental capacity as advanced as ours to make their own decision to either; ignore or respond in obedience. I have been a Christian since I was 15, but did not take His voice seriously until I was 25. I started harkening to His call and the seriousness of it only when I was 25 in 2022. I had been living a life sometimes in the world and sometimes for the kingdom. However, it was He who chastised my heart into complete obedience. I heard His voice and I have seen His Face to its full measure, which was when my own heart was set to complete obedience. I then called out to Him and He heard me. He responded by giving me an inner conviction- that the contents of the book of Revelations were to be taken very seriously, including our final redemption and fearing His judgments to come, over a wicked people.

There was no fear in this, but He drove me into His heart with His Perfect love and He showed me, in such a short period of time, what He considers to be an actual Christian. One who serves Yeshua, with full devotion, not willingly sinning but pursuing a RELATIONSHIP with Him above all else. It is then that when you call out to Him, you have the full confidence in your heart that He will respond and guide you each step of the way. God is a God who does not ignore people, including the unsaved. He hears everything and knows everything and sees everything, and even predetermines everything. How do you think unsaved people get saved? They call out to him in repentance with the full willingness to surrender all and allow Him into their hearts. He hears them, as He hears every single microscopic sound wave to the loudest explosion that could ever occur.

Calling to God is a Christian's entry into the faith

"For whoever calls on the name of the LORD shall be saved." – Romans 10:13 NKJV

All humans are entered into this fallen world with the curse of sin hanging over their life. Like it or not, that is the reality of existence. However, out of His perfect love and deciding that a solution to sin was needed; God sent His Son, Jesus Christ, to redeem us from this curse and bring us back to our loving Father in Heaven. In order to redeem us: Christ lived a perfect life and knew no sin, then was crucified and presented Himself to God as a sacrifice for the sins of all mankind born and yet to be born, died and rose again 3 days later to conquer death and the curse of sin.

The Bible explicitly says that the only way for a person to be saved is to call unto the Lord for salvation and the forgiveness of sins and choosing Christ to be Lord over their life. Now, a key note, is that Christ will never force His way into anyone's life. A person who is ready and aware of their need to be forgiven, will make that decision willingly, by confessing that Jesus is Lord and believing in their heart that God raised Him from the dead.

The key action one person must take is the profession of their faith- which is also calling unto the Lord Jesus to save them. By calling on Him, one is then born again into the faith and has entered into fellowship with the Father, Son and Holy Spirit.

When I was 15, I was invited to a church by my best friend at that time. I didn't see anything wrong and I thought it would be nice to go. I previously came from a Sikh and Buddhist background. A kind man, who is now my close friend and someone who has mentored me for a long time in the faith, approached me and presented me with a Gideon's Gospel of John pocket bible. That action changed my life.

I read the entire Gospel of John and I cannot explain why I believed it to be true, but I just knew deep down that "this was the way" and I continued to go to church. Until one Sunday, I was determined to surrender my life to Christ at an altar call and I did so.

If at any time in this book, you feel convicted or want to give your heart to Jesus to save you, I implore you to read OUT LOUD the following-

> *Lord Jesus Christ of Nazareth,*
>
> *I believe You are the Son of God and I believe God raised you from the dead. I ask you to come into my life right now as I surrender myself to You wholeheartedly. Please be Lord of my life and cleanse me of my sins. Please bring me into Your Kingdom, save me from death and hell, and reveal Yourself to me. In Jesus Christ Name I thank you for Your salvation. Amen.*

Calling to God produces a healthy dependence.

"For I, the Lord your God, will hold your right hand, saying to you, 'Fear not, I will help you.'" - Isaiah 41:13 NKJV

This Bible verse is God clearly letting us know that He will always help us. He is more than willing to hold our hands in every thick and thin situation if we would depend on Him. He commands you not to be afraid but to take the leap of faith on calling and depending on Him.

Would you cast away your pride and surrender all of your dependence on Him today? When life is going well, we forget God. When life is troubling, then we tend to maybe even remember God. Every time something bad happens, even the unbeliever cries out "Oh my God", or "Oh Lord". We as fallen human beings are prone to making mistakes no matter the levels of our intellect. We have to be honest with ourselves because sometimes, we literally have NO ONE to depend on. This leaves room for the Perfect Father, in His Perfect Wisdom to hold our hand and lead us through the worst of storms.

We have to personalize **Isaiah 41:13 NKJV** to our circumstances. **"For I, the Lord your God, will hold your right hand, saying to you, 'Fear not, I will help you."**

Your Father in Heaven is willing and able to support you 24 hours a day out and 365 days a year forever. If you partner with Him on this, you are choosing to walk with Him as He holds you. Imagine a child, completely depending on their parent to hold their hands to help them walk. It is literally the same way He wants you to depend on Him and develop a healthy dependence on Him.

The healthy believer cries out "Oh Lord, My God", in awe and reverence at the start of their day till the time they fall asleep. They trust that God would harken His ears to their cries and they trust Him to guard them every single minute of the day. It is their faith in their dependence on Him which causes Him to move and meet them halfway.

Whenever I call to Him, no matter the time, I can feel and hear Him respond to me in my spirit. This is healthy for me because I know that I have Him to depend on if all else fails. He desires to have this healthy dependence from each and every one of us. He enjoys our dependence on Him because He designed us to depend on Him from the very start.

Consider the verse in **Matthew 18:3: "Assuredly, I say to you, unless you are converted and become as little children…" NKJV**, where Christ points out that all believers must liken themselves to little children when coming to the Father. Little children depend a whole lot on their parents. If you understand this concept, then you are on the way to understanding how to have a healthy relationship with Him.

Calling to God builds character

"But also for this very reason, giving all diligence, add to your faith virtue, to virtue knowledge, to knowledge self-control, to self-control perseverance, to perseverance godliness, to godliness brotherly kindness, and to brotherly kindness love." – 2 Peter 1:5-7 NKJV

When we decide to walk with Christ and have perfect communion with the Father, you might notice certain changes about your personality traits, your speech, your attitudes, or your character. You might find yourself, sooner or later, becoming inwardly transformed. This is the work of the Holy Spirit who comes to live inside of you when you receive Christ into your heart.

One goal of the Holy Spirit is to redevelop your character into the likeness of Christ's character, throughout a period of time, depending on how much the believer yields to the Holy Spirit daily. Over time, we learn more about Christ's characteristics as we study the Word of God and call unto the Father in prayer (recommended daily).

The Holy Spirit imparts into our spirit, through supernatural workings and intellectual knowledge based on reading the Word, the way we should conduct ourselves as good followers of the faith. The overall goal of the Father is to liken each and every child of God into the characteristic of Christ. The reason for this is because Jesus Christ came to represent the characteristics and the nature of God the Father, acting as our perfect role model, so to speak. Jesus testified to his follower Phillip: **"Jesus said to him, "Have I been with you so long, and yet you have not known Me, Philip? He who has seen Me has seen the Father; so how can you say, 'Show us the Father'?" – John 14:9 NKJV.**

Consider this phrase – Like Father, like son.

The fruits of the Spirit are what God expects each believer to begin to grow within themselves, with the help and inward working of the Holy Spirit. **"But the fruit of the Spirit is love, joy, peace, longsuffering, kindness, goodness, faithfulness, gentleness, self-control…." – Galatians 5:22-23 NKJV.** These are the traits and the characteristics of Christ revealed to all mankind who have not seen Him, but believe and want to recognize His character.

Yielding to the Holy Spirit is key in this process because Christ does not force anything on us. We must be willing to be surrendered to Him in each area of our lives. He wants to reveal His nature in us humans because He wants to use His children to reveal His Glory. When unsaved people recognize believers and see the fruits of the Spirit, they are able to get a glimpse of the goodness of God and thus, God willing, winning them over to the kingdom.

Calling to God in trials builds character, especially that of resilience. It increases the faith of the believer, after experiencing God's ability to take a believer through the trial. Trials and tribulations are something the gospel guarantees that believers will go through at some point(s) in their walk with Christ. God allows people to go through certain things so as to shape that person for His glory or to improve a certain trait within that person. Trials also allow us to examine ourselves and get rid of characteristics that may not actually be serving Him or doing us any good.

The character we carry affects us a lot more than we think. If we reflect love, then we walk in His nature. However, if we reflect hatred or bitterness, then we make ourselves miserable and this is not God's will for our character. Hatred, bitterness, unforgiveness and the likes of these are not of the kingdom and can actually destroy our lives. Keep in mind that God wants to change our character so we can enjoy abundance and peace in our lives.

I used to have suicidal thoughts, self-esteem issues and fear of lack. However, when I decided to call to the Lord and yield myself to the Holy Spirit, I found the Lord doing an accelerated work in me to change the way I think. Now, I know how to combat suicidal thoughts and self-esteem issues, using scripture as I receive them from the Lord, if I get them. As a result, the Holy Spirit has developed a sound mind in me. He has given me peace in my daily life. He has taught me to weaponize scripture against the fiery darts of the enemy. I have developed the ability to trust in God to counteract the fear of lack by choosing to believe that He will supply all of my needs according to the riches of His Son Christ Jesus. Knowing that He is my Father and that He will provide all the needs of His children, I have complete trust in Him at every turn and have obtained perfect peace.

Calling to God allows for a deeper revelation

"'Call to Me, and I will answer you, and show you great and mighty things, which you do not know.'" – Jeremiah 33:3 NKJV

If you want to know the secret things of the Heavenlies then you must call unto the Creator of the Heavenlies. God allows His people to know the secrets of His Kingdom through His Son Jesus. When He was incarnate on the earth, He attempted to explain to His disciples that the secrets of the Kingdom could be known by man, if they would submit to God, through Christ His Son, and establish a firm foundation on Him.

Revelation is an ongoing process. When you establish a relationship with Jesus and then decide to deepen that through relentless pursuit of His heart, He continues to reveal Himself to you piece by piece. It is like He is leaving a breadcrumb trail throughout your life. Enticing you to continue to seek His divine revelation until you reach the end of the trail, where you find yourself standing before the gates of His Kingdom. That is what God wills to do with each human being existing and coming into existence.

He wants to reveal His nature to us. He wants to pour out His love and show you every aspect of His Heart through experiences and a relationship with Him. He wants us to know Him as much as our physical mind can comprehend on this earth. He wants you to know and follow the purpose He has designed for your life. He wants you to know many things but majority of revelation comes to us only if we earnestly seek Him wholeheartedly.

Despite this journey of revelation, the enemy will attempt to sway us off course with distractions and try to get into our heads with weaknesses and doubts. This is normal for many believers because the enemy does not want us to know Jesus. If we don't know Jesus, then we lack the strategies of victory over the enemy in the different areas of our lives. God wants you to taste and see that He is good and that comes by revelation. The entire Bible is a revelation of God's love and plans towards mankind.

Revelation from God can come in different forms. Here is what I have experienced:

- I have experienced hearing His voice in my heart and my spirit when I call out to him. **"My sheep hear My voice, and I know them, and they follow Me."- John 10:27 NKJV.** I can hear from Him, because it is my right as His child and I want to live a life pleasing to God. Therefore, I need to hear from Him to receive instructions and guidance. I also can hear His plans for my life when He wants to tell me. I follow His voice to the different areas He has called me and to achieve growth. A key note- you will know it is His voice, speaking to your mind and heart, if the content of the words He speaks align with scripture. His voice can sound like our own internal voice because He sits in our heart and speaks from within. You can save yourself so much grief and heartache in life if you would search for His voice, receive that revelation and follow it. I hear His voice every single day in every area because He is speaking 24/7. It is up to us to adjust our frequency to receive from Him.

- I have experienced seeing images or "visions" when I have practiced the gift of prophecy. When I have prayed diligently and sought Him out through intercession for myself or others, in my mind, images begin to appear, which relate to the topic I am praying about. I usually "see" these images with my eyes closed. I close my eyes to fully concentrate on what He wants to show me and to limit outside distractions. With full concentration on Him, you make room for Him to show Himself and with that greater revelation. I have found the images I see to be accurate as others can confirm that the images shown to me, are able to be received and resonated by the person / people I am praying for, as it matches their circumstances or what they might have seen as well!

- I have experienced dreams from Him; particularly around one theme- my authority. The Lord has given me many dreams throughout the years where in my dream, I am casting out demons or chasing them away. They usually start of with myself taking authority in the name of Jesus Christ, then confronting demons or evil spirits and watching them submit to the authority of Jesus Christ. In this sense, God is giving me revelation of the authority I carry because I am one with His Son Jesus. He has given to all those who believe, to be called the "sons" of God and Jesus Christ had given us all authority to trample over scorpions and serpents. On a general basis- when you are in tune with Jesus Christ, God allows for dreams to visit you in your sleep and often these dreams carry meaning or provide guidance. Some dreams from Him can show you the future. One time, I had been desiring a Godly wife so much, that I had a dream which felt so real, of myself and this woman talking about our plans to have a child. And it felt so good even when I awoke. It was like He was reminding me of His promise to me regarding having a partner.

- Look at the stars in the sky, the way the seasons change, the way animals migrate or move in unison and even study the human anatomy. How everything is specifically designed and formed shows us living evidence that He exists. That is one of His greatest revelations in of itself.

Calling to God in prayer

"But certainly, God has heard me; He has attended to the voice of my prayer." – Psalm 66:19 NKJV

Prayer is an effective tool, the very basic fundamental of every Christian's walk in their life. Besides ingesting and reading the Word every day, prayer is supremely necessary, like breathing, to walk as a Christian. Prayer is not just about asking for things and hoping God will give them. Prayer is a form of partnership through communication with God.

When Jesus walked this earth, we can see from the gospel accounts that He was always praying in a quiet place. He was always talking to His Father before doing His works. God expects the same from us. He wants us to talk to Him, to reach the vantages of Heaven by calling out to Him in prayer. Many people have different constructs to prayer. Jesus simplified speaking to God and said to pray this way as a starting point –

"In this manner, therefore, pray:

Our Father in heaven,
Hallowed be Your name.
Your kingdom come.
Your will be done
On earth as it is in heaven.
Give us this day our daily bread.
And forgive us our debts,

**As we forgive our debtors.
And do not lead us into temptation,
But deliver us from the evil one.
For Yours is the kingdom and the power and the glory forever. Amen."**
– Matthew 6: 9-13 NKJV

"Our Father in Heaven", is how we should start our prayer by acknowledging our God who hears us. He is the recipient of our prayer and we are calling out to Him.

"Hallowed by your Name", is acknowledging that His name is Holy because He is Holy!

"Your Kingdom come", is an agreement we make with Him to establish His Kingdom and its values and righteousness on this earth.

"Your will be done", is the basis on which I live my life and all Christians should live their lives. We stand in agreement that no matter what happens on this earth, God is going to do what He wills anyway. Look at the ending of the book of Revelation – that will give you an idea that God is going to have the final say in the events of the world. GLORY HALLELUJAH, PRAISE BE TO THE KING OF KINGS AND LORD OF LORDS.

"On earth as it is in heaven", is our desire to have the way things running on this earth to be likened to how Heaven is being run. We want the peace, safety and security of Heaven, but more so, we want the presence of God to fill every part of this earth, the same way it fills Heaven.

"Give us this day our daily bread", is asking for Him to provide us our daily needs and refreshments from the resources of Heaven.

"And forgive us our debts, as we forgive our debtors", is something that Jesus Christ requires us to do. We are called to repent as much as we can, daily, by asking for forgiveness for our errors on a daily basis. Then we also ought to forgive those who have wronged us, so that we can experience true liberty from hatred, in our walks. Trust me, you need to forgive others if you want God to forgive you. Jesus Christ specifically addressed this topic and told believers that He requires us to settle our issues with the people around us before presenting a sacrifice before God. God will clean us when we try to clean ourselves. Rely on the Holy Spirit to help you to forgive and confess any unforgiveness to Him directly. Watch how the Holy Spirit works on your heart.

"And do not lead us into temptation, but deliver us from the evil one", is our method of calling Him to help us resist all forms of temptation. God will not allow temptation to overcome us if we are submitted to Him. We can overcome the enemy daily by the blood of Jesus Christ and the Word of our testimony. Trust Him to help you to be stronger each time you resist temptations. He will always give us a way out. It is up to us whether we choose to take it or not.

"For Yours is the kingdom, the power and the Glory forever", is our confession that He is the Supreme Ruler over all things and all things are subject to Him. No matter what calamity or darkness takes over, everything, even the demons are subject to Him and all will bow at the Second Coming of our Lord Jesus Christ, like it or not. His kingdom will never end.

Try to pray the above prayer daily, even as a non-believer, and watch how God responds to you in your life. He wants to reveal His Glory to you through the model prayer that Jesus Christ gave to us.

We also have our own way of praying, but Matthew 6: 9-13 is a good model if we do not know how to pray. It can be seen as a starter point. I remember when I was 15 years old and I was telling someone about Jesus Christ. She was a non-believer at the time but was open to learning how to pray. I taught her the Lord's prayer. After quite some time, I asked her how she went. She said that despite being a non-believer, she had received peace and she claimed to feel better about dealing with her life issues! How amazing!

When you pray, you must trust and believe that God has heard your prayer and will act on it. Sometimes the answer to our prayer can depend on the motive of our heart, from which we pray. We need to regularly check ourselves and see if we are praying with good motives and lining up with His will. **1 John 5:14-15** says, **"Now this is the confidence that we have in Him, that if we ask anything according to His will, He hears us. And if we know that He hears us, whatever we ask, we know that we have the petitions that we have asked of Him" NKJV.** So go ahead and say your prayers daily and watch how His Glory is revealed in your life through your unique circumstances. He is a God who hears everything, including prayer, so you can believe and have assurance that He will answer you.

 ## PRAYER POINT

Father in Heaven. I call to You in the name of Jesus Christ and I ask that You would reveal Yourself to me immediately. Today I want to experience the glory, the power and the Kingdom of God at hand in my life. Father, would You open my eyes and show me Your love and Your plans for me. I ask for a deeper conviction and revelation of Your glory that I may bear witness to Your goodness and mercy.

Father I am here. Please show Yourself to me. Help me to depend on You.

By the power and name of Jesus Christ your Risen Son, Amen

CHAPTER 2

Eyes To See and Ears To Hear

If we want to see and hear the Glory of God, we need to receive power from heaven for our spiritual eyes and ears to be opened. The two most frequent methods which I have seen His glory are through seeing His Divine Revelation and by hearing His divine voice. This is all done through the divine help of the Holy Spirit and by submitting to Him daily. The Lord wants us to have eyes to see and ears to hear because He wants us to encounter His Glory and hear His voice. He wants us to see the secrets of His Kingdom, which is a vital part of our journey to go deeper and deeper in Him.

By faith we believe in what is unseen and the Lord is pleased with that. Isn't it incredible that He does not leave Himself unseen to us individually, if we express to Him that we want His glory to be revealed and His voice to be spoken over us? When we stand in partnership to receive from Him, He will see it through on His end to give to us.

Revealing His Glory to us in unique personal ways, in which He expands our faith in Him, causes us to grow bolder to journey with Him through the valleys and mountains of our lives. When I saw Him for the first time, I could not believe that I saw Him. His face was shown to me naturally as I did my best on my end to pursue Him. Ever since then, I see Him always with His Glory light because He is in His glorified state. This has produced such great faith in me, that even now, if I ever wanted to rebuke the Christian faith and dare to say He does not exist, I cannot even do so, knowing full well He is REAL and I have seen Him personally.

People can discredit the Christian faith and say it is all made up or not real, but one day, when Jesus Christ returns to this world on the clouds of glory, the whole world will see Him and recognize He is King, whether they like it or not and will regret that they never knew Him. Do not be that person, I implore you, today is the day of salvation. Receive Jesus Christ now and I promise, you will encounter Him uniquely in your life.

Consider Mark 4:11-12:

And He said to them, "To you it has been given to know the mystery of the kingdom of God; but to those who are outside, all things come in parables, so that 'Seeing they may see and not perceive, and hearing they may hear and not understand; Lest they should turn, and their sins be forgiven them.'" NKJV.

This passage describes that the mysteries (secrets) of His Kingdom are there for every human to access, however, depending on the state of their heart and faith. They would either fully comprehend this divine revelation as their heart is in the right place (soft enough), or, they would just hear it and not be able to make sense of it because they do not want to make the effort to pursue and understand Him.

Pursuing Him and having the Holy Spirit brings about clarity and understanding so that all passages of the Bible can be understood supernaturally by the inward working of the Holy Spirit on a person's heart and mind. It all comes down to the state of a person's heart. Are they willing to humble themselves to be teachable, so that they can understand the Bible and its messages, or are their hearts too hardened to the truth of His Word that they are not willing to let go of their views and allow Jesus Christ to present Himself?

When the heart is open to the understanding of His Word, Jesus Christ desires that all His people look to experience the unseen realm of His Kingdom. Why would you pursue the things of this earth, which can be lost, stolen, and is decaying day by day, when you could pursue and invest in heavenly treasure and find your place in His Kingdom which will never end?

Put it this way, I could spend 30 years of my life going after money and gold and make that my priority above everything else. After I have finally received all the money and gold, I might enjoy it for one month and the next day after that month, I get into a fatal accident and die. Did my money and gold prevent that from happening? O, you foolish man, why did you waste 30 years pursuing something which can never be carried with you out of this world? Where are the possessions that I sought after 30 years of my life? GONE, just like that, taken without warning! Worldly pursuits will never serve you in the life after death.

Jesus speaks of this in **Luke 12: 15-21 NKJV-**

And He said to them, "take heed and beware of covetousness, for one's life does not consist in the abundance of the things he possesses."

Then He spoke a parable to them, saying: "The ground of a certain rich man yielded plentifully. And he thought within himself, saying, "What shall I do, since I have no room to store my crops?"

So, he said, 'I will do this: I will pull down my barns and build greater, and there I will store all my crops and my goods. And I will say to my soul, "Soul, you have many goods laid up for many years; take your ease; eat, drink, and be merry."'

But God said to him, 'Fool! This night your soul will be required of you; then whose will those things be which you have provided?'

"So is he who lays up treasure for himself, and is not rich toward God."

Are you able to comprehend that the pursuit of riches can be in vain, especially taken after selfish ambition?

Consider this verse-

"If then you were raised with Christ, seek those things which are above, where Christ is, sitting at the right hand of God" – Colossians 3:1 NKJV

The reason Jesus Christ is wanting His people to seek the things above is because He wants us to pursue Him above all else FIRST. You must seek His Kingdom first and everything else will be provided to you, from His Hand, thereafter. As you seek Him wholeheartedly, He will give you a supernatural peace about your life. Do not fear, take the leap of faith and watch as He catches you and translates you into a new realm of seeing and hearing from Him.

Most of what Jesus Christ reveals to us is revealed on a personal level, that which requires a personal relationship to develop understanding and interpretation.

If you want to see into the Heavenly realm, God requires you to focus on Him first. You need to develop a habit of pursuing Him in His Word and worship. He requires your undivided devotion. You cannot serve two masters. "Seeing" into the heavenly realm came to me naturally. I received prayer from a prophetic apostle for my "spiritual eyes to be open" and for the "scales of my eyes to come off" so that I could see into the spirit.

Over a long period of time after that, I could not see anything, but when God called me to operate and practice in the prophetic (as is every believer's right), and as I prayed fervently, I would get mental images or pictures regarding what I was praying about. In this manner, I have seen Heaven, I have seen Jesus Christ, I have seen His throne and many treasures of the kingdom. I also get to see a lot when I spend time in the presence of the Lord in worship or "soaking".

Soaking, based on my experience is where you sit still in a quiet space, shut off from the distractions of the world to spend time with God in your secret / private space. Establish your secret place, it could be in your house or anywhere where there is privacy and quietness. Then, invite the Spirit of God into the space and verbally tell Him that you want to sit in His presence. In this almost meditative state, close your eyes and focus on seeking Jesus Christ from your heart. Let go and let the Holy Spirit take over, then images or pictures might come to your mind.

Do not over analyse anything but take note of these things and pray over them, because you always need to check and confirm with the Lord. If it is from Him, He will make sure you know in your heart of hearts that you saw what He wanted you to see. This can take time and a lot of practice, depending on how much you surrender your time and efforts to Him, but also take note that you must let go of your own efforts and allow God to carry you. Flow with the river and float on it. If God wants you to see something and show His Glory to you, rest assured you will see it if you operate according to His Will.

Trust me when I say this, God really wants to communicate with you and show you His Father's loving heart for you.

If you want to hear from the Most High, you can learn to do so in the "soaking" method which I just covered. As you sit in His Presence, verbally ask Him to speak and pray for your ears to hear what He wants you to hear. I had to practice this and I first heard from Him when I was 18 years old. I used to only be able to hear from Him during my quiet soaking times but over time, as I continued to train my ears to be sensitive, I literally cannot stop hearing Him, no matter if I am driving, brushing my teeth or walking my dog.

Whatsoever you hear in your soaking time, you need to write it all down. Once you have exited that quiet space, you need to pull the content apart and attempt to align it with the content of the Word. Every time that God speaks, it is aligned with that is written in the Word. If you are hearing something that cannot be found in any page of the Bible, discard it immediately, do not be discouraged, and try to hear again.

An example of what I heard God say to me was: "You are my precious son, and in you I am well pleased. I take delight over you." I wrote this down and I looked for similar references in scripture. Does this sound familiar? Examples of this can be found in scripture, such as in **Psalm 2:7 NKJV "...The Lord has said to Me, 'You are My Son...'"** and in **Zephaniah**

3:17 NIV ".... He will take great delight in you..." The more you read the Bible and meditate on scripture, the quicker you will be able to discern His voice, and be able to differentiate lies from the truth.

Notice that what He speaks is in line with what He has said in scripture, and then can be applied to you as you listen for his voice. We need to sit in a quiet space as the Bible commands us to be still and know that He is God. As you practice hearing Him, and if you decide to develop your prophetic gift, ask Him to help you in this area, then you can become a more effective tool for Him to use to encourage other people. You can give people prophetic words about what God wants to do in their life and trust me it can bless many people. I still refer to prophetic words that people have given to me more than five years ago! Ensure that everything is written. Go ahead and create records and files if you need of what God has spoken to you.

Trust me, you need to see and hear from Him to have an advantage in your walk so that you can grow and learn to trust in Him indefinitely, no matter what happens in life.

 PRAYER POINT

Father in Heaven. I call to You in the name of Jesus Christ and I ask that you would reveal yourself to me immediately. Lord, I just ask You to lay Your Hands on my eyes and my ears that they would open immediately to the knowledge of your Heavenly realm. Father, I cry out to you to see You and to Hear from you accurately.

(If you have anointing oil, just dab some on the top of your earlobes and on your eyelids, if not then continue to pray the following)

Lord, I ask for your Heavenly oil and I ask that You would personally anoint my eyes and my ears. Give me grace and wisdom to discern what I see and hear. I ask that You cover my eyes and ears with Your precious blood and that nothing which is not of You, will deceive me.

Thank you, Lord, that I have access to You and the Kingdom.

In Jesus Christ's name, Amen.

CHAPTER 3A

Yod-Heh-Vav-Heh

יהוה

In the Old Testament, one name of God: YHWH, was revealed to Moses in the book of Exodus. YHWH or Yahweh, which comes from the Hebrew word "I AM"; involves the consonants of Yod, Heh, Waw, and Heh, and is also known as the tetragrammaton. God revealed His Name to Moses so that Moses could identify with the God of Abraham, Isaac and Jacob. Over the course of the events of the Bible, God had been identified with many different names such as Adonai, Elohim, Jehovah and El-Shaddai.

The God of the Old Testament is the same God Who exists today and exists within the Trinity of Father, Son and Holy Spirit. In the first days of existence, this same Yahweh created the world in six days and rested on the seventh. He is the one who gave the 10 commandments, flood the world to start anew, gave Abraham one of the greatest inheritances any human could possess. Yahweh worked wonders in the Old Testament amongst His people and displayed His powers to move the heavens and the earth in such a way that if you were alive during those ages, you would know that He was truly the One True God, through Whom all things exist.

Creation, Noah, Abraham, Joseph and YHWH

It all started with the creation of the world. As we explore the book of Genesis, we can see the glory of God revealed in the beginning by the actions of speaking existence into being. God created the heavens and then the earth. Everything that God creates is living, including the Earth. He then spoke light into existence, which we see as the day time light, then the land and the seas. He filled the world with trees, plants and herbs, all of which were capable of sustaining life. He then created a greater light; the sun, and the lesser light; the moon. He filled the seas and the lands with living creatures and commanded them to multiply.

He then moved onto the masterpiece- mankind, which he created in His own image from the dust of the Earth as male and female. He breathed His Breath unto the first created humans and there was life in them. He saw that mankind was good, and being pleased with them, he gave the first two humans dominion over all that exists over the Earth and they co-existed with all created life in the garden of Eden. Even God walked with them in the garden. This is the kind of relationship that God wants to have with you. He wants to, in all His Glory, walk with you in your daily life. The one thing that ruined this relationship between the man, Adam and God was that Adam was disobedient and ate of the fruit of the tree of the knowledge of good and evil, following Eve who was deceived by the serpent. This exact plot is what the enemy wants to cause in every person's life today. This resulted in Adam and Eve being kicked out of the garden of Eden and cursed to live a fallen life on the Earth.

God addressed the serpent's evil temptation in **Genesis 3:14-15 NKJV "So the Lord God said to the serpent: "Because you have done this, you are cursed more than all cattle, and more than every beast of the** field; on your belly you shall go, and you shall eat dust all the days of your life. And I will put enmity between you and the woman, and between your seed and her Seed; he shall bruise your head, and you shall bruise His heel."** This is the first point of reference in history to the coming of the incarnate Son of God and His address to dealing with and overcoming the evil of the enemy. God already had a plan for the future generations, from the garden itself.

As the genealogy of Adam began to expand, and the children of their children multiplied, mankind grew wicked in their ways, finding themselves in all sorts of actions and rituals which were not pleasing to God. This grieved God severely and God decided that He had to start fresh with mankind, because if He let mankind continue in their ways, they were going to ruin the world which God created with their evil intentions. Therefore, He found one righteous man in Noah during those days, and told Noah to create an ark. The purpose of this was to save Noah from God's upcoming wrath on the world and to preserve the first created animals by taking seven clean and two unclean animals of each kind, along with him on his ark. This shows us that despite God's anger on mankind's wickedness, He still loved His creation enough to want to save what was still good in His sight. After the flood had subsided and the ark reached solid ground, God made a covenant with Noah that He would never again flood the earth to destroy living creatures or mankind. As a reminder of His covenant, He placed the first rainbow in the sky. The same rainbow you might see today or tomorrow, is the same rainbow He showed Noah. Mankind and the animal kingdom were once again blessed to multiply and fill the Earth.

Abraham

Moving on, we come across Abram. God spoke to Abram to go out and claim a land that God was going to show Him. God promised Abram that his name would be great. Abram left his home and journeyed with God. God showed His faithfulness to Abram along the way by continuously showing up for Abram as he came across obstacles in his journey. Abram witnessed God destroy Sodom and Gomorrah; two cities which were plagued with the same kind of wickedness that existed on the Earth before God caused the flood. God made a new covenant with Abram and changed his name to "Abraham", because God promised he would be a father of many nations. God essentially set Abraham up to reveal Himself to his descendants all the way down to the present age today. From Abraham would come kings of the earth and many nations, and along with that; the covenant that God would reveal Himself to all Abraham's descendants.

God in all His Glory, very much wanted to walk with His creation despite their failures and weaknesses. He wanted His creation to know Him throughout the descendants of one righteous man. Abraham interceded for a wicked city asking God to spare some righteous people amongst the wicked, and God was moved by Abraham and permitted only a handful of righteous people to be saved before He destroyed the city. God tested Abraham's faith by telling him to sacrifice his son Isaac. Abraham was willing to give up his only son but God stopped Him at the last moment and was pleased with his faith. God is moved when we have faith and especially pleased when we are willing to give up the closest things to us for Him.

Jacob

A story which really interests and moves me is the one of Jacob wrestling with God. Literally! Jacob was the grandson of Abraham and at one point in his life, he was in trouble with his family. His brother Esau wanted to kill him and his uncle Laban was wicked to him. Jacob had fled these people and sought refuge in a spot in the desert. Jacob knew his brother was on the way to kill him, so he had separated his family and sent them away with all his possessions. Jacob then remained alone in the desert until a strange figure made Himself apparent. It is here we note that God came in the form of a "man" and began to wrestle with Jacob throughout the night, until the morning when the "man" struck a blow to Jacob's hip causing an injury, but Jacob still held on and continued wrestling because he knew in his heart, that the "man" he was wrestling with was actually God. Jacob wrestled with him because he wanted a blessing, or help, from God and was not actually willing to let go, until he had seen God come though on a blessing. When they stopped wrestling in the morning, God was pleased with Jacob and changed his name to Israel; which generally means "one who wrestles with God.". Although Jacob would walk with a limp for the rest of his life, he was content that he saw God face to face and God came through on his blessing. This is evident as by the time his vengeful brother caught up to him, instead of killing Jacob, he chose to receive Jacob gladly with favour. God was moved to bless him because he saw that Jacob was not willing to give up on receiving a blessing from God, despite what he had to do. Jacob showed courage and great faith and God was pleased.

Joseph

The story of Joseph is a story which depicts how God can raise up one man to glory, through trials and persecution. Everyone's life is filled with ups and downs and Joseph was one such man who was tested and persecuted for what God placed into his heart. God raised Joseph up greatly because despite the numerous setbacks, he was faithful to God's call on his life. It all started with a dream that Joseph had. It reflected that God had destined Joseph to have a position of reigning with great authority. His brothers were already jealous that their father loved him the most, so imagine the tremendous jealousy which grew to hatred, when Joseph told his brothers that he was going to have authority over much. So, one day, as their hatred grew to manic, his brothers conspired to kill him and throw him in a pit, but one brother suggested to fake his death and sell him off to some traders passing by, who were on their way to Egypt. They tore his tunic from him and dipped it in goat's blood to make it look believable to their father, who wept bitterly, thinking that Joseph had died but was actually sold off. Joseph was taken to Egypt and sold to Potiphar, the captain of the guard for the Pharoah.

Joseph was taken to the house of his new master to work, but the Lord God went with him and prospered his work ethic, so that the master raised him to be the overseer of the property. This was until his master's wife attempted to seduce him day after day, until one day, where she tried to force him to lie with her and stripped his garment from him. Joseph had honour and did not want to sin against God, so he ran away. The master's wife framed him and told everyone that Joseph was the one who was seducing her, showing his garment which was stripped from him to back up her lies. The master was furious and sent Joseph to the Pharoah's prison. Another setback! Once again, the Lord God went with Joseph and gave him favour amongst the guards, so that they gave him a position of authority over the other prisoners and whatever work he did as a prisoner, God prospered him. Pharoah's butler and baker were also condemned to the same prison as Joseph for offending the Pharoah. These two men had dreams and Joseph offered to interpret their dreams. The interpretations came to pass as Joseph had said and they recognized Joseph as someone who could interpret dreams. When the butler was restored to the Pharoah three days after his imprisonment, he forgot about Joseph.

So, Joseph remained in prison for two long years, being faithful, until one day, Pharoah had dreams which could not be interpreted by any of his wise men or magicians. The butler recalled that Joseph could interpret and told the Pharoah, so Pharoah summoned Joseph to interpret the dream. Joseph explained and glorified God in the process, that the dream meant to serve as a warning from God of years of prosperity in the land, followed by famine and that someone would be needed to help the land prepare for these events.

Pharoah saw Joseph as wise and that God was with him, so he immediately gave Joseph the position of governor, which was second in charge over all Egypt and honoured him.

During the years of prosperity, Joseph exercised his authority righteously and prepared for the years of famine. During the famine, under Joseph's wisdom, food was distributed to people who came from all regions to Egypt. Pharoah saw that his dreams had come to pass and I can imagine he was thankful that he gave Joseph authority. In the land of his affliction, Joseph was blessed by God and raised up to a high standard, because he glorified God and remained faithful. At each fall, God came through with a blessing for Joseph. Joseph's brothers, who previously betrayed him, after all these years, sought to go to Egypt to purchase bread due to the famine. When they came before Joseph who was in charge of distribution, they did not recognize him but he recognized them.

He showed mercy to them and invited them to have dinner with him, which is when he revealed himself to them. They were grieved in their hearts and realized their wrongdoing, but Joseph wanted his father to know he was alive. So, joseph commanded his brothers to go back to their land and bring their father to him in Egypt. Joseph's father, who could not believe he was alive, along with his brothers and their families went to sojourn in Egypt under Joseph. Joseph presented them before the Pharoah and they were blessed to stay in the best of lands in Egypt. Upon the passing of their father, Joseph forgave his brothers and explained to them that in their wrongdoing, God changed it around to work it for good.

The story of Joseph shows us that even in the pits, God will remember us and cause us to be blessed wherever we go, if we remember Him and are faithful to Him. He will even cause our wrong doers to be blessed if we, who have His favour, want God to bless them.

 PRAYER POINT

Father in Heaven. I call to You in the name of Jesus Christ and I ask that You would give me the faith of Noah, Abraham and Joseph.

Lord, call me out as a righteous person amongst the wicked, and lead me to build what You want me to build, like You did with Noah.

Lord, lead me, credit my faith in you, bless my descendants, like You did with Abraham.

Lord, cause me to prosper and raise me up, according to Your will, like you did with Joseph.

All in all, I honor the lives of these people and I honor Your Lordship over their lives. Father, raise me up to serve You greatly, for the sake of the lost and lead me into all righteousness.

In Jesus Christ's name, Amen.

Moses and YHWH

The book of Exodus commences by looking at the peril of the Hebrews in the land of Egypt. The Hebrews had lived with Joseph under the old Pharoah until Joseph went to be with The Lord and a new Pharoah had taken over the old one. The new Pharoah was not as kind and open-hearted compared to the old one who knew Joseph. In his cruelty, he looked down on the Hebrews, seeing them objects to use to build and develop the land of Egypt. He suspected that if the Hebrews continued to multiply in numbers, over time, they would take over Egypt or worse, join the enemies of Egypt and turn against all Egyptians. The Pharoah did not want the children of Israel to multiply, lest he could not control their population, so he ordered for the newborn sons to be killed but the newborn daughters to be kept.

One special Hebrew son was born, and his name was Moses. His mother feared he would have to be killed, so she created a makeshift basket for him and set him to float away on a river, in hopes that someone else would take him far away and raise him. It just so happened that Pharoah's daughter was somewhere downstream and saw this makeshift basket floating. She decided to investigate and saw baby Moses in it. She knew the ordeal of being a Hebrew newborn son and had compassion on him. So, she called his mother to nurse him in secret for some time and then officially adopted him as her own child. God chose Moses for His divine plan, and provided safety for Moses, from the very beginning of his life.

When Moses was grown up, he saw an Egyptian man hitting a Hebrew man, who at that time were in bondage and slavery. Moses took pity and ended up killing this Egyptian. The Pharoah found out and wanted to kill Moses, so Moses was forced to flee to a land called Midian. This is where he met a man named Reuel, by helping his daughters in drawing water and defending them from shepherds who tried to drive the daughters away. The man gave him one of his daughters to be his wife and Moses was content to start a new life and live there for a long period of time. Meanwhile, in Egypt, life was getting worse for the Hebrews in bondage and they cried out to God. God heard their cries and remembered the generational covenant He made to their forefather Abraham. God sought to deliver them and had Moses on His mind to execute His perfect plan.

One fine day, as Moses was tending to his flock, God appeared to him in the form of a burning bush. Moses investigated the bush as he thought it was interesting that the bush itself was not burning up to crisps. As Moses investigated, a voice came out of the burning bush and it was God Himself, who introduced Himself as the God of his forefathers and told Moses of his great call to liberate the Hebrews from the bondage of the Egyptians. God gave Moses an articulate plan of leading His people out of slavery and assured Moses that He would handle what Moses could not- in this case being the oppression of the evil Pharoah. He also supernaturally equipped him to perform miracles by the power of God. Moses was also told that Aaron, his older brother, would accompany him and assist him in this task.

Moses and Aaron then made their way back to Egypt, knowing that there was no immediate danger and approached Pharoah to ask that the Hebrews be let go of their duties for three days to worship their God. Pharoah took this as an opportunity to make the lives of the Hebrews more strenuous, forcing them to meet certain quotas in their construction work, because he felt that they were idle in their work, seeing as they had time to "complain" to their God, instead of focusing on their tasks. Moses then question God and complained that He had made their situation worse.

God instructed Moses to speak to Pharoah again and ask for the release of the Hebrew people. God warned Moses that Pharoah's heart would be made hardened so that God would use this to perform more miracles and wonders in favour of the Hebrews. Moses and Aaron then went to Pharoah again and demonstrated the power of God by having Aaron throw down his rod. His rod turned into a snake before Pharoah. Bewildered by this, Pharoah instructed his magicians and wise men to throw their rods, and they also turned into snakes. However, the snake which was Aaron's rod previously ate all the other snakes. What a display of God's power! by this sign, Pharoah's heart was hardened and he refused to grant the release of the Hebrews.

Moses was then told by God to warn Pharoah that God would send plagues to Egypt. It began with the first plague: where God turned the rivers and waters all over Egypt to blood, as Moses struck the river with his rod. Pharoah was still hardened and refused to obey. Then, there was the second plague which resulted in frogs coming out of the river in a countless horde, leaping around the Egyptian's houses and buildings and dying all over the land of Egypt. The third plague came in the form of lice coming upon all the people of Egypt, followed by the fourth with a horde of flies.

It was at this moment that Pharoah spoke with Moses and Aaron to make an intercessory sacrifice to God far away to cease the plagues, so that he would heed in letting the Hebrews go. Moses and Aaron sacrificed to God and God was faithful in ceasing the plague, but Pharoah's heart grew hardened at the last minute again and refused to let the Hebrews go. This resulted in the fifth plague which resulted in all livestock in Egypt dying, except for the livestock owned by the Hebrew people. Then God sent the sixth plague which resulted in horrendous boils over the bodies of the Egyptians. God warned Moses to warn his people to take cover from the seventh plague, which came in the form of tremendous hailstones which caused severe death and damage in the land of Egypt. It was before the final plague, where Pharoah's people and servants begged Pharoah to let the Hebrews go. They had been through enough and could not afford more pain. Pharoah spoke with Moses and Aaron again and threatened that severe evil would follow them if they had left Egypt with all of the Hebrews.

God caused the eighth plague which came in the form of locusts, and they covered the entire land, eating all of the green and fruits out of the land. They came upon the Egyptians in their households and caused them anguish. As a result, Pharoah asked Moses and Aaron to intercede again on his behalf and beg for forgiveness, which they did and God ceased the plague again. Again, once the plague was ceased, Pharoah hardened his heart in the last minute and refused to let the Hebrews go! Therefore, God caused the ninth plague in the form of darkness over the land for 3 days.

It was so dark that no one could see each other and this caused them to remain in place.

God told Moses that there was a tenth and final plague remaining, since Pharoah was not letting the Hebrews go. God caused his Angel to strike down all Egyptian firstborns in the night. God warned his people, through Moses, to cover the doors of their homes with the blood of an unblemished lamb, as a sign of protection, so that the Angel of the Lord would 'pass over' the houses. This is where God commanded the day of "Passover" to be observed every year amongst the Hebrews, passed down to their future generations, as an everlasting ordinance. Once Pharoah's firstborn and all the rest in the land of Egypt who were not protected were struck down, there was a great cry in the land.

At this point, the Egyptians realized it was best to send the Hebrews away. The Hebrews, on their way out, plundered the land of Egypt, by God's approval and favour, and then commenced the mass exodus into the wild. The entirety of them were numbered around 600,000, not including children. The Lord God led the Hebrews through the wilderness in the form of a pillar of a cloud by day, and a pillar of fire by night. The Lord led them to camp near the Red Sea, where around the same time, the Pharoah, who still harboured a hardened heart, decided to chase them and capture them again. When the Egyptian army were nearing their camp near the Red Sea, the came relentlessly as the Hebrews were trapped with no escape. They were being hard pressed against the sea as their backs.

To save them, God displayed His power by parting the Red Sea for the Hebrews to cross through, on dry ground, to get to the land on the other side. Pharoah in his pride, followed them through the partition with his army. Once the Hebrews reached the other side, God destroyed the Egyptians who were caught in the midst of the sea by returning the waters and they came upon those caught in the middle. The Hebrews witnessed the power and the glory of their God and revered Him and his servant Moses. God kept His Word and delivered them out of bondage.

God continued to lead the Hebrews in the desert and performed miracles to sustain them and their faith in Him. He did this by making bitter waters in the desert to become sweet so they could drink from it, by supernaturally making meat and bread appear for them in the desert so they could eat, by causing water to flow from a desert rock to satiate the thirst of the 600,000 and by giving victory to the Hebrews in a conflict which was caused by their enemies in the desert.

After three months in the desert, they approached the area of Sinai, where God called Moses upon Mount Sinai, where the presence of the Most High covered the mountain in a thick cloud, surrounded by lightning and thunder. This is where God revealed the 10 Commandments to Moses upon tablets and instructed Him to teach his people to live according to the 10 laws. God was very strict with these laws but promised protection and His faithfulness upon His people if they were obedient. God also commanded Moses to create the Ark of the Covenant to hold God's commandments, so that he and his people would carry the Law of God wherever they went throughout the land.

Now that God had shown His goodness to His people and liberated them, he did not want them to wander around without guidance but to have His Laws to uphold. God wanted to work with His people to create a nation of God-fearing and God-lead people. In the overall context of this book, we can observe that God is a good God who remembers His promises to His people and will fight for and protect all those who belong to Him and are willing to serve Him. What a good God we serve!

PRAYER POINT

Father in Heaven. I call to You in the name of Jesus Christ and I ask that You would use me, like Moses, to lead those in bondage, into the promised land of Your Kingdom. Lord, use me and send assistance to me to carry out Your tasks and purposes in my life. Lord, make me to be a leader and call me up to Your Mountain, that the Glory of God would be revealed to me tangibly, as You revealed to Moses. Make my face to shine as brightly as You did with Moses' face, so that all who look at me will see Your Face.

In Jesus Christ's name, Amen

Joshua and YHWH

At the end of Moses' life, God took him up upon a mountain to show Moses the land that He was going to bring the Hebrew people into. The same land He promised Abraham and all his descendants. Moses breathed his last after looking upon the land and God came and buried him. This is where God took notice of Moses' assistant; Joshua. It was time for Joshua

HIS GLORY

to step into the role of leadership and partner with God in working out the Hebrews movement into the Promised Land. God blessed Joshua and assured him that as He had promised Moses; Joshua would be given all the land he treads his foot upon and no oppression would come against Joshua because God would be with him all of his life.

At this point in time, the Hebrews had formed a hierarchy and society amongst themselves, upholding the Law of God first and foremost. This is because God was preparing these people to form the future nation of "Israel". By this, we can see that God is capable of creating a society of just men and women for His purposes. Joshua was given charge over all these people and they were willing to obey him, as he obeyed and followed the Lord God. Joshua was led to go towards the city of Jericho and its surrounding lands but this required them to cross the river, Jordan. Keep in mind that the Hebrews now had the Ark of the Covenant, which was carrying the tablets of the 10 Commandments. God told Joshua that when the priests carrying the Ark stepped into the river, the presence of God would rest on the river and He would part the Jordan. So, with faith, the Hebrews crossed the river and as God said, when the Ark of the Covenant began entering the waters, the waters split, forming a path for them to cross. God displayed the same power He did before Moses when they had to cross the Red Sea.

Once they had crossed, God appeared to Joshua in the form of a "Commander of the Lord's Army". This being was dressed for battle with a sword in His Hand. Joshua fell on his face. God then spoke to Joshua, as they were camped near the city of Jericho, and commanded him and his people to march around the city walls of Jericho for 6 days, bearing the Ark of the Covenant and to sound their horns. However, on the 7th day, they were to march 7 times and at the end blow their horns loudly and witness God supernaturally crumbling the walls of Jericho. This happened according to their obedience and faith and when they had done their part, God did what He said would happen and they took over the city of Jericho. Joshua's fame was widespread because God was with Him and gave him victory. Notice that Joshua had the upper hand in this because Joshua walked in obedience and faithfulness. This same God and principle exist today and He will give all those who walk faithfully and obediently with Him, victory in all their battles.

God displayed His power through Joshua by making him a conqueror. God gave over the neighbouring city of Ai to Joshua and the Hebrews; in the same way He gave them Jericho. Another city called Gibeon which was a great city, submitted themselves fearfully to Joshua's rule by a peace treaty, because they had heard of Joshua's conquest. When God is on your side, your enemies will submit to you because of God's favour and power in you. Once Gibeon was under Joshua, the five kings of the Amorites, the king of Jerusalem, the king of Hebron, the king of Jarmuth, the king of Lachish and the king of Eglon, gathered their army and set out to attack Joshua at Gibeon. They feared Joshua's conquest over the neighbouring cities and set out to stop it. However, despite their attempt, God intervened and told them that He had already won the battle for Joshua and that Joshua would prevail. This happened as the Lord God said and Joshua was victorious over his enemies. God continued to fashion Joshua into a victorious conqueror as he took over a great number of cities to the South and North of Gibeon. He also took over the cities of the kings which attacked him at Gibeon. Joshua continued his conquest, by the Hand of the Lord and conquered numerous cities in the East and 31 cities in the West.

Joshua's campaign brought forth supernatural victory on all fronts. He was faithful and obedient to the Lord God from the start to the end of his life and God gave him all of the territories and victories according to what God had planned. Through Joshua, we can see the warrior characteristic of God, who fights for His chosen people and gives them victory on all fronts.

The secret to Joshua's victory and success is revealed in the following verse:

"…. But as for me and my household, we will serve the Lord." – Joshua 24:15 NKJV

 PRAYER POINT

Father in Heaven. I call to You in the name of Jesus Christ and I ask that You make me a great warrior like Joshua. Give me favour and divine assistance to conquer the lands, which the enemy has claimed. Lord, show me which lands to conquer and I will go willingly, knowing that Your Grace surrounds me to overcome the enemy, no matter what form he might take. Clothe me in Your armour and raise up a warrior spirit in me. Put me at the forefront as I lead Your people to victory over the evil one. May the sword of the Most High God be in my hand at all times.

In Jesus Christ's name, Amen.

Job and YHWH

There once existed a man who lived in the land of Uz, who was a righteous man that feared God. Job lived with his wife and had 10 children. He had a great number of livestock, was rich in the land and was known as the greatest. Job worshipped God and hated what was evil in the land. Job was good in character and lacked nothing.

One day, the Bible tells us, that Satan presented himself before God. God presented Job before Satan as a righteous man who hated evil. Satan challenged and questioned Job's faith in God, because he felt that Job was only giving glory to God because Job was prosperous and everything was good with him in the land. God began to test the faith of Job by granting Satan power over his possessions, but He did not allow Satan to touch his person.

The test of faith began by God allowing all of Job's livestock to be destroyed, his servants to be killed and for his 10 children to be killed. Job was informed of this by his surviving servants, who were clearly frightened and dismayed. Job immediately tore his clothes, shaved his head and fell to his face, worshipping and giving glory to God. Job acknowledged God as one who gives and takes away. The Bible says that at this news, he did not curse God but blessed His Name.

Satan then went to God again. God was proud that Job still did not curse Him. So, Satan challenged him again and said that if he were to attack Job's person, then surely Job would condemn God. God then granted

Satan to torment Job, but he was not allowed to take Job's life. Satan then went to Job and struck him with painful boils all over his body. Whilst Job sat in his pain, his wife approached and questioned his faith, telling him to curse God for his peril and to die. Still, Job was not moved by peril but explored the notion of accepting good from God and the bad as well. He did not curse God again. Then, Job's three friends came to comfort and sit with him for a week. They did not speak all week.

The week passed and Job began to curse the day he was born. He broke down in sorrow due to his anguish but took it out on himself rather than God. Job believed that his complaining was just and complained to God to cut his life off from the land. He felt that his suffering was without comfort and was longing for it to end. Job began to feel hopeless and weary. two of his friends told him that he should repent of cursing his life and circumstances, and complaining to God. Job then answered his friends by magnifying God's Glory and reiterating His righteous character over the Earth and all circumstances. Job prays to God for relief over his troubles, knowing full well that God is supreme over all circumstances no matter what they look like.

One of his friends began to discuss with Job how the wicked are punished on the Earth, and given the circumstances and looking at what was evidently happening to Job, accused Job of being wicked. In response, Job proclaimed that God's judgments were just and righteous. Job was fully submitted to God's methods and ways. Job proclaimed the glory of God and his Majesty, whilst acknowledging the frailty of mankind. Job knew His Redeemer and kept his eyes on God. He was adamant once again, on keeping his integrity and not sinning or cursing God. This led to Job's friends ceasing their discussion and arguments with Job because they saw that Job believed he was righteous.

Then there came another man, called Elihu, who was angry towards Job because he felt that in all of this, Job held onto his integrity and was using that to justify himself. So Elihu began to teach Job wisdom and encouraged Job to speak out because Elihu was looking to justify Job. Elihu then began to proclaim God's justice and condemn man's self-righteousness. He proclaimed God's goodness in the land amongst man and his majesty. Elihu encouraged the group to magnify God's work, to which there have been many witnesses.

Then, God appeared to Job in a whirlwind. Now it was time for God to speak and He did so first by revealing His Omnipotent Power over the world, over creation and over mankind. Job remained humbled. God then challenged Job and caused Job to think about who could be compared to God's Glory. Job then humbled himself to the point of repentance and recognized that God was supreme over all things. It was God who is able to do everything and nothing could compare to His Omnipotence.

The Glory of God had been physically revealed to Job and Job recognized that in spite of hearing about God all of his life, he actually saw God now face to face. The measure of glory and radiance emanating from God humbled Job into the dust and ashes of the ground. God then turned to Job's friends and was wrathful for not speaking righteous things to Job in his ailment. He commanded his friends to prepare a sacrifice, over which Job would pray over and God would answer and receive it.

When Job had been faithful to pray over the sacrifice, God had mercy on Job and restored all that he lost twofold. God continued to bless Job throughout his latter days and caused Job to gain more riches than he ever did before. This shows us that when we are faithful to God and recognize God's goodness, He will indeed restore to us all we have lost during our sufferings. Sometimes, He allows things to happen in our lives to test our faithfulness and trust in Him. Above all, magnify the omnipotence of God over the Earth and trust in His goodness, no matter how dark or evil circumstances may be. It is He who has the final say after all is said and done and He restores all things to balance.

PRAYER POINT

Father in Heaven. I call to You in the name of Jesus Christ and I ask that You make me filled with the integrity for You, in the same way that Job had. I ask that You would keep me in times of trouble and help me to magnify Your glory over my life and on the Earth. Lord, I thank You that You are long-suffering towards me. I asked for You to keep me strong like Job throughout suffering. I ask for lips that would not sin against You. I thank you, Lord, that You are the one who has the final say in any and all circumstances in my life. I ask that You restore all that was lost to me.

In Jesus Christ's name, Amen.

Isaiah and YHWH

The Book of Isaiah commences with a man, called Isaiah, a servant of God who is given a vision by God, concerning God's displeasure with the cities of Jerusalem and Judah and His Judgement upon them. God had sighted the wickedness within the cities and was condemning it but He was willing to forgive the people who would turn from their wickedness. God wanted to cleanse all the filth away from the cities and establish His Glory upon Mt. Zion, in the form of a cloud of smoke by day and flaming fire by night. From God's standpoint, He utilizes judgment to clean out wickedness and reset the subjects of His judgment. The purpose of His reset is to teach the people of the Earth the error of their ways and provide an example to the consequences of wickedness. God judges very strongly so that the lessons echo from generation to generation.

Isaiah was chosen by God to become a prophet for His Name's sake. He encountered a vision of God in His glory, in the third Heaven, seated upon His Throne in His Heavenly Temple. The Lord was high and lifted up and the train of His robe filled His temple. He was radiating with Glory. Above the Lord's throne stood a few Seraphim, which are six winged angels that surround the throne of God. They were calling God holy, giving Him glory, surrounding His throne and worshipping God. In God's presence, because it was such a holy environment, Isaiah felt unclean. But instantly, one of the Seraphim ministered to Isaiah by taking a piece of coal from the Altar of God and touching Isaiah's lips, rendering Isaiah clean and having been purged of all iniquities. Isaiah was made pure in the house of God. Isaiah heard God questioning out loud who He should send on His behalf to carry out His will and Isaiah was willing and asked God to send him. God told Isaiah to warn the people living in Jerusalem and Judah that God would judge them unless they had repented. Isaiah was made a Prophet in the sight of God and His Holy Angels.

The role of a prophet is to be a physical mouthpiece regarding the communication of God to mankind. Prophets receive revelation from God through their senses, such as: seeing into the spirit realm, hearing God's voice or knowing something is about to happen. With the heavenly information and communication from God, a prophet is led by the Spirit of God to prophesy words of warning or future events to a person or group of people. Practicing prophesy is an accessible gift to ALL born again and spirit filled true Christians and it can be used specially to edify and build up people, to give hope and direction from God.

In Isaiah's case, his first assignment as a prophet was to be sent to king Ahaz, the king of Judah, to give him counsel and to strengthen him, for Ahaz was in the middle of conflict amongst two other kings. Moreover, through Isaiah, the prophecy of the coming of the Son of God was given to Ahaz. Ahaz was also warned that the king of Assyria will conquer the land of Judah and prevail. Isaiah was then given the word of instruction; for the people to obey the laws of God and to fear Him. God turned His words to Israel and began to judge them concerning the wicked, whom He said He would cut off from the land. God said that once His will had been accomplished upon Mount Zion, then He would strike the arrogance of invading Assyria and destroy the invading forces. After all the warfare and destruction would occur, God said that there would be remnant of people in the land of Israel who would once again return to God in repentance, after witnessing His judgements upon the lands, and keep His Law with a newfound faith and reverence.

The Lord God enunciated again the coming of the Son of God, from the root of Jesse, who will stand as a banner to His people. He spoke concerning that one day, where this Son would assemble all outcasts of Israel and Judah and remove their oppositions. And in that, all His people would praise His name for His deliverance and salvation would come to His people. God displays the coming Son's authority over the world in **Isaiah 9: 6-7 NKJV -**

"For unto us a Child is born, unto us a Son is given; And the government will be upon His shoulder. And His name will be called Wonderful, Counsellor, Mighty God, Everlasting Father, Prince of Peace. Of the increase of *His* government and peace *There will be* no end..."

He boldly declares to Isaiah who is to come and how great of an authority He will have over the nations of the world. In **Isaiah 61:1 NKJV "The Spirit of the Lord God is upon Me, Because the Lord has anointed Me, to preach good tidings to the poor; He has sent Me to heal the broken hearted, to proclaim liberty to the captives, And the opening of the prison to those who are bound..."**.

God not only addresses the authority of the coming Son of God, but He illustrates His purpose. The Lord God is a God of hope and remedy and reveals to Isaiah that there is remedy on the way in the form of the Son of God. The purpose of the coming Anointed One is to bring the Good News of God's hope to those who are oppressed and caught up in the curse of sin. Remember that God is a God of mercy and wants all people to be set free and redeemed in Him alone. The Lord prepared a plan for perfect healing through the Son of God, that if they accept the Son, then He would be able to heal them through their faith. God wants people out of any bondage as a result of sin and the coming Son of God would be the breaker of their chains. God's overall plan was a plan of reconciliation and in Isaiah, He provided the hope of this promise so that the people who obeyed God and believed Isaiah's revelatory words; would have something to hold onto. They would have the coming Messiah to wait and hope for.

God then gave Isaiah another prophecy concerning the judgement of the world in the future and the future "Babylon" nation. In this prophecy, God speaks of mustering His Heavenly armies and moving to destroy

Babylon. There would be great fear and peril for the wickedness of the Babylonian nation due to their practices of wickedness. He likened the destruction of their pride as to when He destroyed Sodom and Gomorrah! The Lord God continued to inform Isaiah of the impending destruction against nations such as Assyria, Moab, Syria, Ethiopia, Egypt, Edom and Arabia and a few others. However, He would bless the nation of Israel, Assyria and Egypt, despite His judgment on them, because God could see that in these nations of iniquity, there were righteous people who were willing to stand in the gap of the wicked dwellers and by reminding all who dwelt there, who the Lord was, they would be brought to repentance and find mercy in God's eyes.

God deals fiercely with idolatry amongst the people. If it is one thing God really despises, it is idolatry. He alone is the Supreme Lord of all – **Isaiah 44:6 "Thus says the Lord, the King of Israel, and his Redeemer, the Lord of hosts: 'I am the First and I am the Last; Besides Me there is no God.**

Part of the reasons of God's impending judgment on the nations was due to idolatry amongst the wickedness of the people. God calls idolatry foolish and says that those who make graven images for themselves to worship will not benefit themselves and will amount to nothing. Those who pray to their created idols have a strong delusion upon themselves. They do not have eyes to see and are unable to understand that what they are doing is ultimately praying to a piece of stone or rock, which cannot see or hear their prayers. Moreover, it is not even a living thing, unlike the true God who lives. God specifically addresses that those who pray to idols are not able to deliver their souls from His judgment and are fully deceived, feeding on lies.

Despite God's judgements on nations, we can observe that His eyes were still looking for the few righteous people within to save and to have mercy on. And if these righteous people could stand in the gap and turn even a few wicked to repentance, then He would invoke divine protection on them as He would carry out His judgment on the land. Despite God using Isaiah to deliver prophetic judgements, God spoke multiple prophecies of the coming Son of God who would come and bring hope to His people. He reveals to Isaiah that there will come an end time judgment upon the Earth where the Earth will be made desolate, scattering all the inhabitants and bringing judgment to the wicked people in the high places. All those esteemed in their own pride shall be destroyed. All the high rulers with riches and wealth shall be cast down. He informs Isaiah that at the end of the age, He will descend upon the Mt Zion and establish His rule over all the Earth and over all mankind. In the end time prophecy, He displays His Power over the enemy and tells Isaiah that He will specifically destroy the reptile in the sea called Leviathan! Israel will be restored in its splendour according to the will of God and all His people will worship Him on future Mt Zion. God declares He is the one who will be the Saviour of the nation of Israel at the end and all of His people.

"But now, thus says the Lord, who created you, O Jacob, And He who formed you, O Israel:

Fear not, for I have redeemed you; I have called you by your name; You are Mine." – Isaiah 43:1 NKJV

The Lord God reveals to Isaiah a great deal of the coming of Jesus Christ through references in the Book of Isaiah. If you were to read the New Testament, there are many cross references, even the quotes of Jesus Christ, which match to what God said through Isaiah. Isaiah was observed as a prophet who delivered the warnings of God's judgment but was also given the hope of Jesus Christ who would one day come and redeem the curse of sin over mankind. This shows the mercy and judgment sides of God. Where He knows He must execute judgment to address wickedness, God still looks for those whom He can redeem. He knew that mankind needed a Saviour and that a holy people and nation needed to be established through Israel for Him to dwell amongst on the Earth. A lot of which he revealed to Isaiah.

At the conclusion of the Book of Isaiah, we observe that the Lord ends on a high note, reminding us of His precious promises of His reign. When we come before His glorious reign, our hearts shall be filled with perfect joy and our bones shall flourish. We who serve the Lord shall know His hand. Knowing His hand is a sense of knowing Him personally. God is a personal God who wants His people to know Him in a personal and affectionate way. He does not judge the righteous but is interested in developing covenants and a relationship of friendship, support and love with them. However, His wrath will be known to His enemies and all those who have been wicked to the righteous and innocent.

Isaiah gives us a picture that when the Lord comes to reign, He will come in a chariot of fire and display His righteous rebuke with flames of fire. The fire of the living God is that which consumes all sin and uncleanness. He addresses even those who purify themselves but turn to idolatry, that they shall also be cut off in their sin. The Lord knows every person's thought, hearts and ways and will reward or judge them accordingly. He shall set signs and gather all the nations to come and bear witness to His Glory upon the Earth, and they shall declare His Glory amongst one another. He will gather His people upon His holy mountain, He shall establish His new Heaven and Earth which will remain for Him, and He promises that the names of His righteous people will also remain forevermore. Finally,

He reminds us that his righteous people will bear witness to the decay of the evil and wicked transgressors. This final warning is to serve as a call for repentance for the wicked to come and join the righteous. He is a just God who does not want anyone to perish, however He must also judge justly and all mankind will be allotted their rewards or judgment according to their works.

God has stressed this notion multiple times through Isaiah, which is a means of reiterating the importance of being saved and being counted worthy to come into His dwelling place. Let the words of prophet Isaiah serve as a call to repentance.

 PRAYER POINT

Father in Heaven. I call to You in the name of Jesus Christ and I ask that You help me to heed Your Words of warning, but also remind me of Your Promises of remaining saved under Your Perfect Reign. Father, help me to observe my iniquities and Your righteous judgment towards the sinful and wicked. For You have mercy on the righteous and those who are willing to repent. Father, I thank You that the righteous will remain forever.

(Dear reader, this is a chance for you to be saved because the Lord God is going to have His final say and His rule established at the end of mankind's age. If you want to be saved, pray the following)-

Lord Jesus Christ of Nazareth,

I believe You are the Son of God and I believe God raised You from the dead. I ask You to come into my life right now as I surrender myself to You wholeheartedly. Please be Lord of my life and cleanse me of my sins. Please bring me into Your Kingdom, save me from death and hell, and reveal Yourself to me.

In Jesus Christ's name I thank You for Your salvation. Amen.

Daniel and YHWH

In the days of Daniel, Israel's reigning king was lost in an invasion to king Nebuchadnezzar of Babylon and with it were lost some articles of the house of God. The new reigning king, after conquering the land, instructed the master of his eunuchs to find able bodied men without blemish, to be trained to serve in the king's palace. Among these people was Daniel and his friends. Daniel was not willing to defile himself with the wine or the delicacies of the new king so he requested permission from the head of the eunuchs to be excused from the defiled food of the king. God was with Daniel and gave him favour in the eunuch's sight, but Daniel insisted that he and his friends, who also did not want to be defiled, be tested with a vegetarian diet and then have their appearance examined. The reasoning behind this test was that the eunuch did not want trouble in the king's eyes, should Daniel and his friends become malnourished and not be able bodied to serve the king, and have to answer for it.

After 10 days of testing with a vegetarian diet, with God's favour, they appeared healthier than the other servants who ate and drank from the king's table. God worked on Daniel and 3 of his friends by giving them exceptional knowledge and understanding and Daniel became gifted in understanding dreams and visions. The king even tested Daniel and his friends and found them to be 10 times greater in wisdom and understanding as compared to his own magicians and astrologers. When God chooses someone, He begins a good work of favour and giftings in them from the very start. He causes His chosen to excel and be recognized before others so that they may see something unique and almost "out of this world" in them.

One day, the king had a dream and was anxious to know the meaning of the dream. He threatened to kill his astrologers and magicians if they could not give him the dream's interpretation. They were unable to interpret and out of his fury, the king decreed that all the wise men be killed, inclusive of Daniel and his friends. When Daniel found out of this decree, he approached the king and asked for time to interpret the dream. The king agreed, so he went back to his house and shared this with his friends, and they all asked God for an interpretation of the dream so that they might not die amongst the other wise men. God gave him a vision and revealed the meaning of the dream to him, and Daniel and his friends praised God because they could be saved from death.

Daniel went before the king and interpreted the dream. Daniel explained to the king that no one could interpret the dream other than God, giving God the glory. Daniel explained to the king even the thoughts the king was having about what is to come after his successful conquest. The dream which was revealed illuminated the king's future; concerning kingdoms which would rise up after his current kingdom and they would take over his kingdom. The king was convicted in his heart and being fearful, offered praise to Daniel's God, whom he recognized as God of all gods. Daniel was then promoted to become ruler over all of Babylon and chief over all the wise men of the kingdom. This was the same method God used to promote Joseph, previously in Egypt. This shows us that the same God that was with Joseph was present with Daniel. The God of promotion and exaltation!

Much to the dismay of Daniel, king Nebuchadnezzar built a huge gold idol and set it up in Babylon. He commanded that all the high officials of the nation be present for its dedication and at the sound of the music played, all the people were to fall down and worship this idol. Whoever was not in submission to this command was to be thrown into a fiery furnace. At a certain time, the Chaldean people came to accuse the Jewish people in the land as they worshipped their own God and did not pay their dues to the king or his gods. Outraged at this, the king commanded for three of Daniel's friends Shadrach, Meshach and Abed-Nego to come and bow. With great faith in their God, they did not bow and told the king that the God of Israel would deliver them from their fiery outcome. So, the king commanded them to be sent into the furnace, which was heated seven times more than usual.

(The following part gives me chills!)

The king's men who bound the three into the furnace were caught up in the flames but Shadrach, Meshach and Abed-Nego fell down, in the furnace and called out to God. The fire did not touch the three but the king and all his counsellors in their astonishment and amazement, looked into the furnace and saw a fourth man in there! All four of these men were in no way hurt and the fourth man was described as one in the "form of the Son of God". GLORY TO JESUS!!! He came in His Spirit (before He was meant to come into this world) and protected His three faithful men. The king called these 3 men out and the whole cohort observed that not even the hairs on their head or bodies had been burnt, nor smelled like smoke. Immediately, the king marvelled at their God and sent out a decree that no one was allowed to offend or speak against the God of Israel, the one true God, and then promoted Shadrach, Meshach and Abed-Nego to high positions in Babylon. Read this story for yourself in **Daniel 3** and give yourself time to marvel at His Glory, which was revealed before those who oppose Him and those who were changed after bearing witness to His works.

Soon after, king Nebuchadnezzar had another dream which really astonished him. Being convinced now that Daniel was carrying the Spirit of God, he sent for Daniel to interpret this second dream. When the king told Daniel the dream, Daniel was astonished as well but informed the king that his second dream of a growing abundant tree was representing the king himself, who had grown in power. However, in the dream, a Holy Watcher came and struck the tree down whilst allowing its roots to remain in the ground; which meant for the king that he would be driven from men but his kingdom would remain. It would require for the king to be convicted that it is only the power of the Most High God to give power and take it away and all rule belongs to God alone.

This dream was a form of humbling the king and bringing him down in his pride. The king's pride was hurting as he believed that he had built his own kingdom Babylon with his own power and hands. Then abruptly, a voice from heaven came and spoke to the king reminding him that his kingdom has departed from him and he would be driven into the fields amongst the beasts to eat grass. In that very hour, the exact thing happened and the king became like an animal in the wild, all by himself surrounded by animals. Whilst Nebuchadnezzar was in the wilderness, his understanding returned to him and He gave all glory to God and praised His name. He had been humbled and, in his humility, surrendered his pride before

God and understood that all things and all kingdoms come from the God of Israel first and foremost. At this, God had mercy on him and restored his kingdom back to him. A prominent realization which occurred to Nebuchadnezzar in this ordeal was that God is One who abases the proud and boastful.

Pride leads to destruction and God opposes those who are proud and think they are better than others. God is more than happy to remind all the proud people of the Earth who is actually in charge, and sadly, with the ignorance of many warnings, people learn the hard way, as was the case for Nebuchadnezzar!

Much later in the age, Nebuchadnezzar had a son which inherited his throne, Belshazzar, who was ruling and celebrating one fine evening. He held a feast with his officials and they were celebrating and honouring their own idol gods. The king, in his pride, decided he wanted to drink from the gold goblets, which were taken from the temple of Jerusalem by his father. This was done and as they drank, the pridefully praised idols. Suddenly, a supernatural hand appeared and wrote on a wall near the king's palace. When the king discovered this, his appearance had changed, amidst the joy of their celebration and demanded one of his astrologers, Chaldeans and the soothsayers to interpret the writing. No one could make it out but the Queen who had joined them reminded them that there was a man in the days of the king's father who had the Spirit of God within him: Daniel. Daniel was summoned to give an interpretation and was promised to be rewarded for his time. The king also acknowledged that YHWH was with him, besides possessing excellent wisdom and understanding.

Daniel started by telling king Belshazzar of his father's kingdom, pride and fall until Nebuchadnezzar understood that God was in charge over the Earth and all powers. Then Daniel addressed the sin of the king which was idolatry in their present celebration and then gave the interpretation as a warning.

Daniel 5:25-28 NKJV -

"And this is the inscription that was written:

MENE, MENE, TEKEL, UPHARSIN.

This is the interpretation of each word-

MENE: God has numbered your kingdom, and finished it;

TEKEL: You have been weighed in the balances, and found wanting;

UPHARSIN: Your kingdom has been divided, and given to the Medes and Persians.

The king immediately gave Daniel the third highest position of rulership in the kingdom of Babylon. Unfortunately, that very night the king died and a new king: Darius was granted the kingdom in his stead.

Under the rule of the new king Darius, he appointed multiple overseers with Daniel being amongst them, however Daniel was favoured because of harbouring an excellent spirit and being favoured with God. This caused jealously amongst the other overseers and they sought to find fault in Daniel. At first, they could not find any because Daniel was a faithful governor to the king. So then, the overseers sought to find fault with him concerning the law of his God, YHWH. They consulted amongst each other and established a decree which stated that anyone who petitions with any god or man for 30 days shall be thrown into the lions' den. They were attacking the faith of Daniel because he walked closely with God and that would've meant praying and talking with YHWH every day.

Daniel found out about this decree, which was signed by the king, and went home and gave thanks to God in prayer and fasting. The overseers who conspired against Daniel, spied on him and witnessed him praying. They immediately told the king that he was technically breaking the law by petitioning with God. The king tried all evening, till the morning to work around this new law to deliver Daniel from the consequences, but his overseers informed him that this law could not be changed. The king's hands were tied! As a result, he was forced to send Daniel to the lions' den. Before he sealed the mouth of the den shut behind Daniel, the king gave Daniel a word of encouragement that YHWH would deliver him. This new king, although having his hands tied by his own established law, was wise and revered the Living God. He shut the den up behind Daniel and retreated to his palace, fasting and thinking of the situation all night with no sleep.

The next morning, king Darius went to check up on Daniel, hoping in his heart that YHWH had delivered him. He called out to Daniel and Daniel responded, giving glory to God that an Angel of the Lord had attended to Daniel in the den and shut the mouths of the lions. Daniel came out of the den, and upon examination, was found to be completely unharmed. The king immediately sent Daniel's accusers into the lions' den as he was displeased by their accusations and conspiracies and established a decree that the God of Daniel; YHWH was to be feared and revered by all citizens in the kingdom of Babylon, and gave God the glory. Daniel prospered as the Good Lord of all mankind was raised up in the kingdom of man.

King Darius was a very smart and wise king for fearing God and any politician or ruler in the high places of the kingdom of man would be utterly wise to fear the one true Yahweh, who can establish kings and remove kings according to His will. Let this serve as a warning to anyone who is abusive of their power or filled with pride in a position of great authority.

Daniel was visited with interesting revelation which came in the form of visions and dreams. Look at **Daniel 7: 2-14 NKJV-**

"Daniel spoke, saying, "I saw in my vision by night, and behold, the four winds of heaven were stirring up the Great Sea. And four great beasts came up from the sea, each different from the other. The first was like a lion, and had eagle's wings. I watched till its wings were plucked off; and it was lifted up from the earth and made to stand on two feet like a man, and a man's heart was given to it.

And suddenly another beast, a second, like a bear. It was raised up on one side, and had three ribs in its mouth between its teeth. And they said thus to it: 'Arise, devour much flesh!'

After this I looked, and there was another, like a leopard, which had on its back four wings of a bird. The beast also had four heads, and dominion was given to it.

After this I saw in the night visions, and behold, a fourth beast, dreadful and terrible, exceedingly strong. It had huge iron teeth; it was devouring, breaking in pieces, and trampling the residue with its feet. It was different from all the beasts that were before it, and it had ten horns. I was considering the horns, and there was another horn, a little one, coming up among them, before whom three of the first horns

were plucked out by the roots. And there, in this horn, were eyes like the eyes of a man, and a mouth speaking pompous words."

Then he had a vision of God and the coming of the Son of God.

"I watched till thrones were put in place, And the Ancient of Days was seated; His garment was white as snow, And the hair of His head was like pure wool. His throne was a fiery flame, its wheels a burning fire; A fiery stream issued And came forth from before Him. A thousand thousands ministered to Him; Ten thousand times ten thousand stood before Him. The court was seated, And the books were opened. I watched then because of the sound of the pompous words which the horn was speaking; I watched till the beast was slain, and its body destroyed and given to the burning flame. As for the rest of the beasts, they had their dominion taken away, yet their lives were prolonged for a season and a time. I was watching in the night visions, and behold, one like the Son of Man, coming with the clouds of heaven! He came to the Ancient of Days, and they brought Him near before Him. Then to Him was given dominion and glory and a kingdom, that all peoples, nations, and languages should serve Him. His dominion is an everlasting dominion, which shall not pass away, And His kingdom the one Which shall not be destroyed"

The interpretation of these visions given to Daniel concerning the great beasts were representative of four kings which would arise in the Earth at a certain time. The saints of God would be given victory and authority to receive the kingdom of heaven forever and ever. The last beast which Daniel saw was the beast who would make war with the Saints of God in the end times and prevail for some time, but the 'Ancient of Days' (being God) would step in with judgment against the evil beast and give victory to the Saints.

The fourth beast represented a fourth kingdom which would arise in the Earth but it would be a unique kingdom, in that it would have dominion over ALL THE EARTH, unlike any other kingdom in the Earth which ever was. It would destroy the Earth and its way of life. The ten horns represented 10 kings which would be loyal to this evil kingdom. There would be one specific king after the 10 kings, who would have authority over three of these earlier kings. And this final specific king would persecute the Saints of God and prevail of the Saints for some time. God will then judge this king and take away his dominion forever. Eventually all of these kings and these kingdoms will be given over to God and His people to rule over and this shows that God has the final victory in the end.

Daniel had encountered another vision. Take a look at **Daniel 8 NKJV-**

"I saw in the vision, and it so happened while I was looking, that I was in Shushan, the citadel, which is in the province of Elam; and I saw in the vision that I was by the River Ulai. Then I lifted my eyes and saw, and there, standing beside the river, was a ram which had two horns, and the two horns were high; but one was higher than the other, and the higher one came up last. I saw the ram pushing westward, northward, and southward, so that no animal could withstand him; nor was there any that could deliver from his hand, but he did according to his will and became great.

And as I was considering, suddenly a male goat came from the west, across the surface of the whole earth, without touching the ground; and the goat had a notable horn between his eyes. Then he came to the ram that had two horns, which I had seen standing beside the river, and ran at him with furious power. And I saw him confronting the ram; he was moved with rage against him, attacked the ram, and broke his two horns. There was no power in the ram to withstand him, but

he cast him down to the ground and trampled him; and there was no one that could deliver the ram from his hand.

Therefore, the male goat grew very great; but when he became strong, the large horn was broken, and in place of it four notable ones came up toward the four winds of heaven. And out of one of them came a little horn which grew exceedingly great toward the south, toward the east, and toward the Glorious Land. And it grew up to the host of heaven; and it cast down some of the host and some of the stars to the ground, and trampled them. He even exalted himself as high as the prince of the host; and by him the daily sacrifices were taken away, and the place of his sanctuary was cast down. Because of transgression, an army was given over to the horn to oppose the daily sacrifices; and he cast truth down to the ground. He did all this and prospered.

Then I heard a holy one speaking; and another holy one said to that certain one who was speaking, "How long will the vision be, concerning the daily sacrifices and the transgression of desolation, the giving of both the sanctuary and the host to be trampled underfoot?"

And he said to me, "For two thousand three hundred days; then the sanctuary shall be cleansed."

The Angel Gabriel meets Daniel in this vision and interprets this vision for him:

"Then it happened, when I, Daniel, had seen the vision and was seeking the meaning, that suddenly there stood before me one having the appearance of a man. And I heard a man's voice between the banks of the Ulai, who called, and said, "Gabriel, make this man understand the vision." So, he came near where I stood, and when he came, I was afraid and fell on my face; but he said to me, "Understand, son of man, that the vision refers to the time of the end."

Now, as he was speaking with me, I was in a deep sleep with my face to the ground; but he touched me, and stood me upright. And he said, "Look, I am making known to you what shall happen in the latter time of the indignation; for at the appointed time the end shall be. The ram which you saw, having the two horns—they are the kings of Media and Persia. And the male goat is the kingdom of Greece. The large horn that is between its eyes is the first king. As for the broken horn and the four that stood up in its place, four kingdoms shall arise out of that nation, but not with its power.

"And in the latter time of their kingdom, when the transgressors have reached their fullness,

A king shall arise, having fierce features, who understands sinister schemes. His power shall be mighty, but not by his own power; He shall destroy fearfully, and shall prosper and thrive;

He shall destroy the mighty, and also the holy people.

"Through his cunning, He shall cause deceit to prosper under his rule; And he shall exalt himself in his heart. He shall destroy many in their prosperity. He shall even rise against the prince of princes; But he shall be broken without human means. "And the vision of the evenings and mornings, which was told is true; Therefore, seal up the vision, for it refers to many days in the future."

As Daniel continued to receive these visions, he turned to God in fear and repentance. Daniel began to intercede on behalf of the wicked people in the land. He had great revelation and he wanted the mercy of God to fall on the people. He pleaded with God for forgiveness. The Lord God met him halfway with two prophecies. The first prophecy occurred when Daniel was in prayer to the Lord and the Angel Gabriel appeared to him and gave him the "70-week prophecy" in **Daniel 9: 21-27 NKJV-**

".... yes, while I was speaking in prayer, the man Gabriel, whom I had seen in the vision at the beginning, being caused to fly swiftly, reached me about the time of the evening offering. And he informed me, and talked with me, and said, "O Daniel, I have now come forth to give you skill to understand. At the beginning of your supplications the command went out, and I have come to tell you, for you are greatly beloved; therefore, consider the matter, and understand the vision:

"Seventy weeks are determined, for your people and for your holy city, to finish the transgression, to make an end of sins, to make reconciliation for iniquity, to bring in everlasting righteousness, to seal up vision and prophecy, and to anoint the Most Holy.

"Know therefore and understand, that from the going forth of the command to restore and build Jerusalem until Messiah the Prince, there shall be seven weeks and sixty-two weeks; the street shall be built again, and the wall, even in troublesome times.

"And after the sixty-two weeks, Messiah shall be cut off, but not for Himself; and the people of the prince who is to come shall destroy the city and the sanctuary.

The end of it shall be with a flood, and till the end of the war desolations are determined.

Then he shall confirm a covenant with many for one week; but in the middle of the week, he shall bring an end to sacrifice and offering. And on the wing of abominations shall be one who makes desolate, even until the consummation, which is determined, is poured out on the desolate."

This prophecy held revelation that the Son of God would be coming into the world and Jerusalem, the city of Israel would be built, and later on in the end times of this age, the Anti-Christ would emerge to bring death and destruction. The country of Israel is viewed as God's end time clock, wherein prophetic events that take place concerning Israel give us a rough understanding of how close the return of Christ is to the world and how close the Anti-Christ might be revealed.

The final prophecy which was revealed to Daniel was concerning the End of Time, in **Daniel 12 NKJV-**

"At that time Michael shall stand up, the great prince who stands watch over the sons of your people; and there shall be a time of trouble, such as never was since there was a nation, even to that time. and at that time your people shall be delivered, everyone who is found written in the book. And many of those who sleep in the dust of the earth shall awake, some to everlasting life, some to shame and everlasting contempt. Those who are wise shall shine

Like the brightness of the firmament, and those who turn many to righteousness

Like the stars forever and ever. "But you, Daniel, shut up the words, and seal the book until the time of the end; many shall run to and fro, and knowledge shall increase."

Then I, Daniel, looked; and there stood two others, one on this riverbank and the other on that riverbank. And one said to the man clothed in linen, who was above the waters of the river, "How long shall the fulfillment of these wonders be?"

Then I heard the man clothed in linen, who was above the waters of the river, when he held up his right hand and his left hand to heaven, and swore by Him who lives forever, that it shall be for a time, times, and half a time; and when the power of the holy people has been completely shattered, all these things shall be finished.

Although I heard, I did not understand. Then I said, "My lord, what shall be the end of these things?"

And he said, "Go your way, Daniel, for the words are closed up and sealed till the time of the end. Many shall be purified, made white, and refined, but the wicked shall do wickedly; and none of the wicked shall understand, but the wise shall understand.

And from the time that the daily sacrifice is taken away, and the abomination of desolation is set up, there shall be one thousand two hundred and ninety days. Blessed is he who waits, and comes to the one thousand three hundred and thirty-five days."

But you, go your way till the end; for you shall rest, and will arise to your inheritance at the end of the days."

There is seriously going to be an end-time to the age of man. At the end of all our lives, some of us will go into glory but others will go to destruction, which is also known as hell. Those of us who have served the Lord Jesus Christ will be counted worthy to live in the presence of God and we shall shine like the stars in the firmament. The end of times is a really serious matter and a lot of Biblical prophecy has already been fulfilled in this present age. Carefully watch the signs of the end, anticipate the return of

Jesus Christ and choose carefully for yourself where you want to end up. It will be the best choice you will ever make, should you decide to abide in the Father's arms. All evil will be judged and destroyed, that includes the humans who have not been redeemed or cleaned. Choose carefully.

(I, as the author, have been instructed by the Holy Spirit, to include the prophecies and visions straight from the Scriptures, in a non-summarized format, so that you, as the reader, may truly grasp the seriousness of what is to come at the soon end of the age.)

PRAYER POINT

Father in Heaven. I call to You in the name of Jesus Christ and I ask that You help me to understand the deep wisdom and revelation behind the visions and the prophecies given to Your servant Daniel. I thank You Father that I have been given the opportunity to understand the coming end of the age and I am willing to receive further revelation from You in a more personal manner.

Father, would You reveal more of Yourself to me and examine my heart and life, so that I may understand whether or not I am redeemed and counted worthy to enter everlasting life. Convict me Father, for the end times are a very serious matter and I ask You to please count me worthy that I may escape the hour of trial which is to come upon the Earth.

In Jesus Christ's name, Amen.

CHAPTER 3B

Yeshua

Jesus said to her, "Did I not say to you that if you would believe you would see the glory of God?"- John 11:40 NKJV

We have just examined the prophecies of Yeshua's entry into the Earth through the Old Testament servants and prophets of God. The meaning of the name "Jesus" (in Hebrew: Yeshua) can be attributed to *"Savior"* or *"Yahweh saves"*. The meaning of "Christ" means *"The Anointed One"*. Yeshua's birth was revealed to his natural mother, Mary, by the Angel Gabriel because she was given the honor of birthing the Savior of mankind into the world. Yeshua came into the Earth as a humble babe born in a barn in Bethlehem but hailed from Nazareth. Yeshua preached repentance, love and salvation through Him and Him alone as He claimed to be the prophesied Messiah, the Son of God, Savior of the human race and redeemer of all sinners. Yeshua was all about showing us the glory of God, through His perfect and sinless life. He came to live a perfect life, fulfilling the Old Covenant Mosaic law of God in His perfection and to bear the curse of the Law of sin and death upon Himself, for a beautiful exchange of our sin for His salvation.

Since the time of Adam, sin had found its way into the world and over the course of events explored in the Old Testament, wreaked havoc, misery, pain and death in mankind. The enemy, Satan, introduced sin and exploited mankind as he had the upper hand over the human race, whilst they continually sinned and exchanged into the law of sin and death if they did not heed God. God already had a redemption plan from the Garden of Eden, and began to introduce the coming of the Son of God through His chosen prophets and elect in the Old Testament. Yeshua came to redeem us from the law and curse of sin. From the beginning of the age of His understanding, He knew what He needed to do. At the age of 12, He was found in a temple in Jerusalem by his earthly parents, speaking with the wise men there and they marvelled at Him. He knew that He was to be about His Father's business and His earthly parents knew as well.

Yeshua began His ministry after being baptized by John the Baptist. At the point of emerging from the water, a Voice from Heaven cried out **"This is My Beloved Son in whom I am well pleased." – Matthew 3:17**. This shows us Yahweh's love and confirmation for Yeshua being the promised Son of God and Messiah unto the people. The Holy Spirit, who descended upon Him, led Him to fast in the desert for 40 days, whilst being tempted by Satan. He overcame all temptations and remained pure and obedient to God. Jesus quoted **Isaiah 61:1 NKJV - The Spirit of the Lord God is upon Me, because the Lord has anointed Me to preach good tidings to the poor; He has sent Me to heal the brokenhearted, to proclaim liberty to the captives, and the opening of the prison to those who are bound"**, to illustrate to us the purpose of why He came and what He needed to do for us. Everything He did was FOR us and our eternity.

Yeshua called Himself the True Shepherd. He promised salvation for all of those who would follow and hear His voice and promised He would lead us into eternal life. He called Himself the Good Shepherd who was willing to lay down His life for His sheep, that His sheep might find everlasting life in Him. He also recognized other sheep, who were not of His fold, which he wanted to bring into His fold and give to them everlasting life. He promised that when we as people become His sheep, nothing will snatch us out of His Hand. He promises to lead us as a Good Shepherd and to keep us from destruction.

Yeshua said **"I am the resurrection and the life. He who believes in Me, though he may die, he shall live." – John 11:25 NKJV.** By this, He meant that all who believe in Him, although they succumb to natural death, their spirits shall live forever with Him in Eternal Glory. Through His death on the cross, He purchased the right for us to have eternal life with His Blood being the only currency worthy to overcome the enemy. We will be resurrected once He comes again, where our earthly body, whether in the dust or presently alive, will be joined with our eternal Spirit, so we will receive a completely new and refined heavenly body, so that we can be likened to Him in full.

Examine **John 14 NKJV-**

"Let not your heart be troubled; you believe in God, believe also in Me. In My Father's house are many mansions; if it were not so, I would have told you. I go to prepare a place for you. And if I go and prepare a place for you, I will come again and receive you to Myself; that where

I am, there you may be also. And where I go you know, and the way you know. Thomas said to Him, "Lord, we do not know where You are going, and how can we know the way?"

Yeshua was appealing to the faith of the people who believed in the laws of Yahweh and the story of Moses. He knew that they had the capacity to believe so He challenged their faith to believe that He was indeed who He said He was. He then gave them something to look forward to, which would stir up faith. He spoke of heaven. He promised that if we have faith in Him, He will personally come and receive us to take us home, where we originally came from. This was new to Thomas because Yeshua extended the invitation of going to Heaven personally to His disciples.

Jesus said to him, "I am the way, the truth, and the life. No one comes to the Father except through Me.

Yeshua boldly claimed this truth to convict all people that only by coming into faith and relationship with and in Him, can we have access to the Father in Heaven and His Kingdom. Simply put, there is no other way, method or religion that can bring you to the True God other than by faith and profession in His Lordship.

"If you had known Me, you would have known My Father also; and from now on you know Him and have seen Him."

Philip said to Him, "Lord, show us the Father, and it is sufficient for us."

Jesus said to him, "Have I been with you so long, and yet you have not known Me, Philip? He who has seen Me has seen the Father; so how can you say, 'Show us the Father'? 10 Do you not believe that I am in the Father, and the Father in Me? The words that I speak to you I do not speak on My own authority; but the Father who dwells in Me does

the works. Believe Me that I am in the Father and the Father in Me, or else believe Me for the sake of the works themselves.

Yeshua revealed the intimate nature of the Father. He mimicked the Father so closely; it was as if Yahweh came down and loved and walked with His people. He told people that He and the Father are one. Whatever Yeshua does or thinks, the Father does or thinks and vice versa. He linked His purpose and ministry to the Father's will, to reinforce that it was the Father Himself operating in Him. He established His ministry based on the Father's authority.

Jesus also said in **John 14:9 NKJV- "Have I been with you so long, and yet you have not known Me, Philip? He who has seen Me has seen the Father..."** He tenderly loved all those He came across and had compassion for the broken, poor and suffering people. He healed those who came to Him and professed their faith in Him. He loved the worst of sinners and immediately forgave and delivered them from the bondage of their sin.

There was a woman who was in the sin of adultery. She was brought to Yeshua by the scribes and Pharisees of the temple in Jerusalem. They claimed that according to the law of Moses, this woman ought to be stoned for being adulterous, in fact, she was caught red handed in the very act. They wanted to test Him, so they questioned Him and asked Him what He would have to say about this matter. They were hoping that He would say something contradictory to the law of Moses so they would have an excuse to get Him in trouble. Yeshua responded to them by convicting their consciences **"He who is without sin among you, let him throw a stone at her first." – John 8:7 NKJV.** They were taken aback and began questioning themselves, rather, they began to examine themselves! They realized that they were not perfect either and far from it. Slowly, they dispersed. Yeshua then went to the woman and asked her where her accusers were. She looked around, astonished and saw that every single accuser had left the area. Yeshua loved her and said **"Neither do I condemn you; go and sin no more." John 8: 11 NKJV.**

That is the perfect expression of His love for all of us who have been involved in the deepest and darkest sins, which may cause society to reject and even want to kill us. But He does not condemn us and He wants us to run into His arms and feel His acceptance, His love and His forgiveness. He wants to forgive each and every sinner who would turn to Him and repent of their sins. Often times, when we get caught up in sin, we dig a grave and we go down deeper and deeper into it, which can lead to death. We tend to get caught up in a repetitive and destructive cycle of sin where we destroy ourselves and we begin to believe the lies of the enemy.

This can leave us with a hopelessness mindset because if we think that we are already so bad, then we might as well remain bad because no one would accept us or forgive us. We tend to be hopeless about our sinful situation because we have allowed the enemy to plant seeds of sin in our minds, which can take deep root and grow to become strongholds in a quick amount of time; which begin to take control over our lives.

This has been the enemy's pattern of working for the longest amount of time and he can do it very sneakily. All it takes is entertaining one "small" sin and believing the lie that we have control to stop this sin at any time we want. Before we know it, we become entangled in a web of sin(s) and this can also give way for more sins to be planted and opens the door to further demonic influences over our lives. **"Do you not know that to whom you present yourselves slaves to obey, you are that one's slaves whom you obey, whether of sin leading to death, or of obedience leading to righteousness?"- Romans 6:16 NKJV.**

Yeshua came to break these mindsets, or strongholds, and all the years of sinning and hiding in the darkness. He came to pull us into the light and restore us wholly and completely, abiding in the light of His love and redemption forevermore. He is more than willing and powerful to deliver us in the snap of His fingers, but all it takes for us is to be willing to surrender our brokenness, filth and bondages to Him. **"For you were once darkness, but now you are light in the Lord." – Ephesians 5:8 NKJV. "He has delivered us from the power of darkness and conveyed us into the kingdom of the Son of His love…" – Colossians 1:13 NKJV.**

Jesus worked miracles in His life to display the power and glory of God. Matter of fact, He carried out a lot of miracles which led to witnesses immediately believing in Him and following Him. The miracles He did were empowered with the glory of God and they were FOR the people involved. The reason for His miracles were to show people who He said He was and to display the power of God, to those who believed in Him. One of His glorious miracles were when He fed 5000 people with 5 loaves of bread and 2 fish. This can be seen in **John 6: 1-13 NKJV-**

"After these things Jesus went over the Sea of Galilee, which is the Sea of Tiberias. Then a great multitude followed Him, because they saw His signs which He performed on those who were diseased. And Jesus went up on the mountain, and there He sat with His disciples.

Now the Passover, a feast of the Jews, was nearby. Then Jesus lifted up His eyes, and seeing a great multitude coming toward Him, He said to Philip, "Where shall we buy bread, that these may eat?" But this He said to test him, for He Himself knew what He would do.

Philip answered Him, "Two hundred denarii worth of bread is not sufficient for them, that every one of them may have a little."

One of His disciples, Andrew, Simon Peter's brother, said to Him, "There is a lad here who has five barley loaves and two small fish, but what are they among so many?"

Then Jesus said, "Make the people sit down." Now there was much grass in the place. So, the men sat down, in number about five thousand. And Jesus took the loaves, and when He had given thanks He distributed them to the disciples, and the disciples to those sitting down; and likewise of the fish, as much as they wanted. So, when they were filled, He said to His disciples, "Gather up the fragments that remain, so that nothing is lost." Therefore, they gathered them up, and filled twelve baskets with the fragments of the five barley loaves which were left over by those who had eaten."

Could you imagine that sight? Yeshua looked to heaven and gave God the glory, knowing full well that the Father was working in Him to win these people over with His miracles, signs and wonders. He promises us that if we faithfully follow Him, we get to partake in these miracles, signs and wonders, and even greater things; bearing witness to His perfect nature and glory.

Another miracle that Yeshua did was that He healed a woman with the issue of blood. We can explore this in **Mark 5:25-34 NKJV-**

"Now a certain woman had a flow of blood for twelve years, and had suffered many things from many physicians. She had spent all that she had and was no better, but rather grew worse. When she heard about Jesus, she came behind Him in the crowd and touched His garment. For she said, "If only I may touch His clothes, I shall be made well."

Immediately the fountain of her blood was dried up, and she felt in her body that she was healed of the affliction. And Jesus, immediately knowing in Himself that power had gone out of Him, turned around in the crowd and said, "Who touched My clothes?"

But His disciples said to Him, "You see the multitude thronging You, and You say, 'Who touched Me?'"

And He looked around to see her who had done this thing. But the woman, fearing and trembling, knowing what had happened to her, came and fell down before Him and told Him the whole truth. And He said to her, "Daughter, your faith has made you well. Go in peace, and be healed of your affliction."

This woman must've had some of the worst 12 years of her life. You could imagine that during that time, she would've tried every avenue of healing but to no avail. When she heard of the Messiah passing through town and His miraculous works, there would've been one last spark of faith left in her to get herself healed. She channelled all the hope and faith that she could and dared to touch the garment of Yeshua to receive her healing.

Did you notice that in this account, Yeshua did not go up to her and find her to heal her, but rather she took the gigantic leap of faith to trust that He was Son of God capable of all healing.

Yeshua's response was the admiration of her faith. He credited her faith, rather than His personal touch, for the healing of her sickness. This is the kind of faith we need to have to receive our healing. This woman's account was the display of the requirement of faith that one needs to have to receive healing for whatever they need. 12 long and troublesome years, she must've thought there was nothing else she could do. But the Son of God stepped in and changed her life completely. This is the kind of change that Yeshua intended to bring to the broken and sick people. This is so that the people who were touched and are presently being touched by Him today, can have their sparks of faith and hope in Him stirred up to their maximum potential, resulting in them professing that He is the Son of God.

In His ministry, Yeshua spoke a lot concerning heaven and hell. Heaven and hell are real places of the afterlife. We live in this temporary body and every person has the Breath of God in them and also a Spirit or "inner man", which is an eternal being, meaning it lives forever. God sent Yeshua down to warn us of the dangers of entering hell and rebuked us in our sins to stay away from that place. He also offered heaven to each of us. He has informed us to **"Enter by the narrow gate; for wide is the gate and broad is the way that leads to destruction, and there are many who go in by it. Because narrow is the gate and difficult is the way which leads to life, and there are few who find it. - Matthew 7:13-20 NKJV.**

He informed us what we are to expect if we are to pursue Heaven, but also showed us how easy it is to perish in hell, if we are not careful. Yeshua was tremendously serious on the topic of the afterlife because we have to choose where we spend eternity. Some of us might have a long time to decide but for others, tomorrow is not promised. We do not have the promise of time because anything can happen to us at any time which can cause us to go to one of these places. Yeshua explicitly stated that He is the only way to paradise. It is so easy to end up in hell that we do not even have to try, because of the issue of the law of sin and death, with which each one of us are born into. If we are redeemed by Him, that law no longer applies to us and qualifies us to enter into Glory. Yeshua was sent to become the bridge itself, for mankind to reach Heaven. There is no other way!

"Nor is there salvation in any other, for there is no other name under heaven given among men by which we must be saved." – Acts 4:12 NKJV

Yeshua assured people that He would go and prepare a place in the House of God for all those who believed in Him. There is peace, joy, safety and immeasurable Glory. There is no pain in heaven, no death, no sickness. Everyone lives in pure and eternal joy in the presence of God, Yeshua and all the holy angels. Everyone has an inheritance in heaven which they get to enjoy personally. There are many gifts and rewards catered to people individually, based on their faith and how well they served Yeshua on this earth. I don't know about you, but I want to go to the Father's arms, where I know, I will never have to feel depression, anxiety, pain, disappointment, suffering of any nature, loss, grief or any temptations ever again. When we believe in and make Yeshua Lord of our lives, we trade in our death inheritance and receive a reservation in the glorious Kingdom of Heaven, which is continuously expanding and growing as more people enter into glory daily. Yeshua personally loves us in heaven and we get to spend time and get to know all the characters of the Bible, the angels, all the other people (saints) who have gone before and even saved family and friends; who will be reunited with us in a perfect paradise.

The Scriptures warn us of the horrors of hell. Please keep in mind that Yeshua does not send us there, we CHOOSE to go there. This is because we are still living under the law of sin and death, and if we do not choose to get an antidote but continuously live an unrepentant life, based on the free will that God has given us, then we cannot enter into the presence of God with the sickness and stains of sin in us. As a very unfortunate result, and it pains me writing this, we end up in the abode of the demons. Hell was originally created for the devil and his angels because they SINNED. God is a just God and He cannot tolerate sin, there has to be some sort of penalty- **"They will be punished with everlasting destruction from the presence of the Lord and from the glory of His power" - 2 Thessalonians 1:9 NKJV**

This factually spells out eternal separation and damnation, where if you end up there, you will never get to experience any form of pleasure or joy. Worst of all, the presence of God will be shut out forever from an eternally dark place of pain and suffering. **"....and those who practice lawlessness,** and will cast them into the furnace of fire. There will be wailing and gnashing of teeth." – Matthew 13: 41-42.

The people who are in hell call out to God because they finally understand what they missed out on. In their pride, they thought they would make it to heaven or they simply did not believe. They received their reality check but it is too late because once you go there, you can never cross over to Heaven. Imagine, a gruesome torment that NEVER, EVER ENDS. Repent NOW before it is too late. Every time a soul goes into hell, Yeshua weeps because He came to save them through His death and resurrection, but still that soul rejected Him. He already gave the only solution to eternal life, but they chose eternal death and, in their pride, thought they could find their own way there. There is simply no other way.

Look at this account in **Luke 16:19-31 NKJV-**

"There was a certain rich man who was clothed in purple and fine linen and fared sumptuously every day. But there was a certain beggar named Lazarus, full of sores, who was laid at his gate, desiring to be fed with the crumbs which fell from the rich man's table. Moreover, the dogs came and licked his sores. So it was that the beggar died, and was carried by the angels to Abraham's bosom. The rich man also died and was buried. And being in torments in Hades, he lifted up his eyes and saw Abraham afar off, and Lazarus in his bosom.

(Abraham's bosom represents heaven and Hades represents hell).

"Then he cried and said, 'Father Abraham, have mercy on me, and send Lazarus that he may dip the tip of his finger in water and cool my tongue; for I am tormented in this flame.' But Abraham said, 'Son, remember that in your lifetime you received your good things, and

likewise Lazarus evil things; but now he is comforted and you are tormented. And besides all this, between us and you there is a great gulf fixed, so that those who want to pass from here to you cannot, nor can those from there pass to us.'

Abraham addresses the gap in the middle of Heaven and hell where neither can cross over to each other!

"Then he said, 'I beg you therefore, father, that you would send him to my father's house, for I have five brothers, that he may testify to them, lest they also come to this place of torment.' Abraham said to him, 'They have Moses and the prophets; let them hear them.' And he said, 'No, father Abraham; but if one goes to them from the dead, they will repent.' But he said to him, 'If they do not hear Moses and the prophets, neither will they be persuaded though one rise from the dead.'"

In this last segment, you can see that the rich man, although prideful on earth, was humbled by the conviction of the horrors of hell. There was no escape and he finally knew how real the horrors of hell were. He was living them day and night, and will continue to live them throughout eternity. Please avoid this place at all costs. Be saved by believing in the name of the Son of God who did everything necessary to bring you to heaven. There is no other way.

When the time for Yeshua to bear the cross was nearing, He felt it and knew that it was time for Him to bear the ultimate sacrifice. He prayed in the Garden of Gethsemane in the early hours of the morning before the day of His sacrifice. You could imagine the overwhelming feeling of dread He felt because He knew what He had to endure, not just physically, but emotionally, psychologically, but most of all spiritually. He knew He had to bear the weight of the sins of all mankind upon His shoulders and His body and give up His perfect sinless life to bear the burden of the world.

"Then Jesus came with them to a place called Gethsemane, and said to the disciples, "Sit here while I go and pray over there." And He took with Him Peter and the two sons of Zebedee, and He began to be sorrowful and deeply distressed. Then He said to them, "My soul is exceedingly sorrowful, even to death. Stay here and watch with Me."

He was filled with dread as mentioned before. He wanted His disciples to remain near in one of His most vulnerable points in His life as He confided in them what He was experiencing.

He went a little farther and fell on His face, and prayed, saying, "O My Father, if it is possible, let this cup pass from Me; nevertheless, not as I will, but as You will." Then He came to the disciples and found them sleeping, and said to Peter, "What! Could you not watch with Me one hour? Watch and pray, lest you enter into temptation. The spirit indeed is willing, but the flesh is weak."

Again, a second time, He went away and prayed, saying, "O My Father, if this cup cannot pass away from Me unless I drink it, Your will be done." And He came and found them asleep again, for their eyes were heavy.

So, He left them, went away again, and prayed the third time, saying the same words. Then He came to His disciples and said to them, "Are

you still sleeping and resting? Behold, the hour is at hand, and the Son of Man is being betrayed into the hands of sinners. Rise, let us be going. See, My betrayer is at hand."

Notice that as much as He wanted to not go through with it, He knew it was the will of His Father in heaven and He kept God's will the main focus and the first priority in His life. Examine yourself, if you are faced with adversity despite knowing that God wants you to experience something, would you still be willing to deny your fleshly desires and go through with it? This is what Yeshua dealt with but He understood that He would triumph and emerge victorious for eternity. It was the price He was willing to pay, if it meant that out of His love for us, He could have us saved from death and hell. This is why Yeshua died for YOU and me and His love for us drove Him to bear the cross for YOU and me.

After Yeshua prayed, He regrouped with His disciples. Then along came Judas, His betrayer, who brought with him a detachment of troops, and officers from the chief priests and Pharisees and they came there with lanterns, torches, and weapons to arrest Jesus. The Pharisees wanted to arrest because they were one of the biggest oppositions to His ministry and everything that He had been doing. They claimed He was blasphemous to claim to be the Son of God and did not believe He was the Messiah. They were sick of Yeshua challenging their belief in God and trying to expose the imperfections of the pride of the Pharisees. Judas greeted Yeshua with a kiss, as a signal to highlight Yeshua out to the soldiers, and he was arrested straight away. Judas was awarded 30 pieces of silver for selling out Yeshua.

Yeshua was brought before the High Priest who questioned Him. **John 18:19-24 NKJV-**

"The high priest then asked Jesus about His disciples and His doctrine.

Jesus answered him, "I spoke openly to the world. I always taught in synagogues and in the temple, where the Jews always meet, and in secret I have said nothing. Why do you ask Me? Ask those who have heard Me what I said to them. Indeed, they know what I said."

And when He had said these things, one of the officers who stood by struck Jesus with the palm of his hand, saying, "Do You answer the high priest like that?"

Jesus answered him, "If I have spoken evil, bear witness of the evil; but if well, why do you strike Me?"

Then Annas sent Him bound to Caiaphas the high priest."

By this point, a majority of His disciples had dispersed and Yeshua was on trial by Himself. Peter, however, followed the crowd and kept an eye on the questioning from a distance. Sadly, when Peter was questioned for following Yeshua by people in the crowd; 3 times he denied ever knowing the Son of God. When Peter realized that he had denied Yeshua, according to what Yeshua told Peter; that he would be in denial, then saw it had come to pass, Peter ran away in his shame and guilt.

"Then they led Jesus from Caiaphas to the Praetorium, and it was early morning. But they themselves did not go into the Praetorium, lest they should be defiled, but that they might eat the Passover. Pilate then went out to them and said, "What accusation do you bring against this Man?"

They answered and said to him, "If He were not an evildoer, we would not have delivered Him up to you." Then Pilate said to them, "You take Him and judge Him according to your law."

Therefore, the Jews said to him, "It is not lawful for us to put anyone to death," that the saying of Jesus might be fulfilled which He spoke, signifying by what death He would die.

Then Pilate entered the Praetorium again, called Jesus, and said to Him, "Are You the King of the Jews?"

Jesus answered him, "Are you speaking for yourself about this, or did others tell you this concerning Me?"

Pilate answered, "Am I a Jew? Your own nation and the chief priests have delivered You to me. What have You done?"

Jesus answered, "My kingdom is not of this world. If My kingdom were of this world, My servants would fight, so that I should not be delivered to the Jews; but now My kingdom is not from here."

Pilate therefore said to Him, "Are You a king then?"

Jesus answered, "you say rightly that I am a king. For this cause I was born, and for this cause I have come into the world, that I should bear witness to the truth. Everyone who is of the truth hears My voice." Pilate said to Him, "What is truth?" And when he had said this, he went out again to the Jews, and said to them, "I find no fault in Him at all." – John 18: 28-38 NKJV.

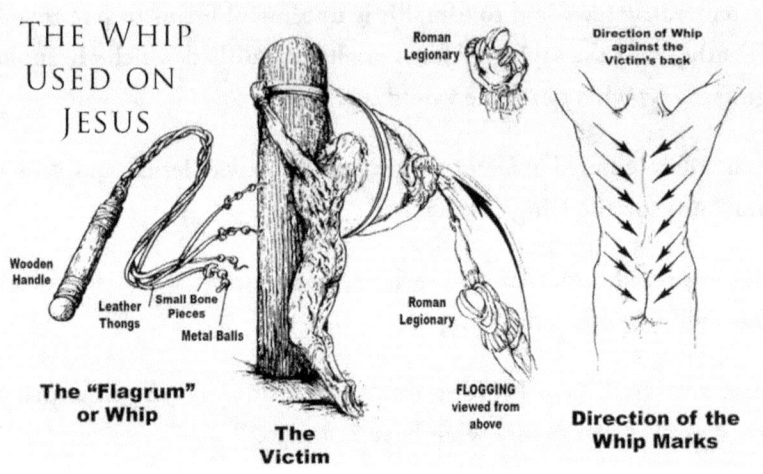

Pilate thought it would appease the Pharisees to flog Yeshua and to let that be the end of it. So, he was taken to be flogged, and the soldiers mocked him, hit him and affixed a "crown of thorns" upon His head. It was a supremely painful moment and Yeshua suffered major blood loss and other physical ailments. Pilate then presented Yeshua to the crowd and told them he found no fault in Him.

"Then Jesus came out, wearing the crown of thorns and the purple robe. And Pilate said to them, "Behold the Man!"

Therefore, when the chief priests and officers saw Him, they cried out, saying, "Crucify Him, crucify Him!"

Pilate said to them, "You take Him and crucify Him, for I find no fault in Him."

The Jews answered him, "We have a law, and according to our law He ought to die, because He made Himself the Son of God."

Therefore, when Pilate heard that saying, he was the more afraid, and went again into the Praetorium, and said to Jesus, "Where are You from?" But Jesus gave him no answer.

Then Pilate said to Him, "Are You not speaking to me? Do You not know that I have power to crucify You, and power to release You?"

Jesus answered, "You could have no power at all against Me unless it had been given you from above. Therefore, the one who delivered Me to you has the greater sin."

From then on Pilate sought to release Him, but the Jews cried out, saying, "If you let this Man go, you are not Caesar's friend. Whoever makes himself a king speaks against Caesar." When Pilate therefore heard that saying, he brought Jesus out and sat down in the judgment seat in a place that is called The Pavement, but in Hebrew, Gabbatha. Now it was the Preparation Day of the Passover, and about the sixth hour. And he said to the Jews, "Behold your King!"

But they cried out, "Away with Him, away with Him! Crucify Him!"

Pilate said to them, "Shall I crucify your King?"

The chief priests answered, "We have no king but Caesar!"

Then he delivered Him to them to be crucified. Then they took Jesus and led Him away. – John 19: 5-16 NKJV.

As you have read, the angry mob of the Pharisees and the rest of the crowd, which were being stirred up by the enemy, demanded Yeshua's death. They even provoked Pilate by stating he was not loyal to Caesar if he released Yeshua. Pilate sought to release Yeshua, but He knew that He had to go through with the events leading to the sacrifice so He did not dispute His case. Pilate then washed his own hands clean of the death of Yeshua and delivered him to the crowd. They then gave him an old, rugged cross for Him to carry as the crowd followed, mocking, laughing, cursing and mourning over Him.

John 19: 17-19 NKJV - "And He, bearing His cross, went out to a place called the Place of a Skull, which is called in Hebrew, Golgotha, where they crucified Him, and two others with Him, one on either side, and Jesus in the centre. Now Pilate wrote a title and put it on the cross. And the writing was:

JESUS OF NAZARETH, THE KING OF THE JEWS.

On the cross were two thieves, one cursed Him as He hung amongst them, whilst the other believed He was the Son of God and repented on the spot.

Then one of the criminals who were hanged blasphemed Him, saying, "If You are the Christ, save Yourself and us."

But the other, answering, rebuked him, saying, "Do you not even fear God, seeing you are under the same condemnation? And we indeed justly, for we receive the due reward of our deeds; but this Man has done nothing wrong." Then he said to Jesus, "Lord, remember me when You come into Your kingdom."

And Jesus said to him, "Assuredly, I say to you, today you will be with Me in Paradise." - Luke 23:39-43 NKJV.

Even as Yeshua was suffering, He was looking to save those who repented and believed in Him. That was why He allowed for himself to be on the cross in the first place- to fulfill the exchange of sin for salvation.

After this, Jesus, knowing that all things were now accomplished, that the Scripture might be fulfilled, said, "I thirst!" Now a vessel full of sour wine was sitting there; and they filled a sponge with sour wine, put it on hyssop, and put it to His mouth. So, when Jesus had received the sour wine, He said, "It is finished!" And bowing His head, He gave up His spirit. – John 19: 28-30 NKJV

Yeshua had completed the sacrifice and the exchange of sin for salvation, therefore He committed Himself into the Father's hands and breathed His last. This was God's sacrifice for us- **"For He made Him who knew no sin to be sin for us, that we might become the righteousness of God in Him." – 2 Corinthians 5:21 NKJV.**

His disciple Joseph and a rich man Nicodemus took down His body, prepared it for burial and sealed His body in a tomb. The disciples, all scattered, were distraught thinking that they had failed. They did not understand that what was about to take place, would display the ultimate victory over death.

Three days later, Yeshua rose from the dead, being resurrected by the Father and officially dominating death and hell. He now held the keys to Hades and overcame the enemy. His sacrifice and His mission to save us was now complete, rendering the law of sin and death void. Take note that He also came to redeem us from the law of God under the Old Covenant because it was impossible for man to keep the laws of God and not break one. If one law was broken, then the person who broke that was guilty of breaking all of the laws. He was worthy enough to redeem us from the law because he had fulfilled the law in His life. Thus, through His death and resurrection, the new Covenant was established and this applies to all believers in today's age. We sit under the agreement of mercy and forgiveness with God because Yeshua died for us.

Yeshua then went to meet with His disciples and all those who followed Him closely and dwelt with them for some time. He performed more signs, miracles and wonders. The disciples had a newer level of faith and their spirits were restored. Yeshua restored Peter, after denying him. By this point Judas the betrayer, had committed suicide out of guilt.

"And truly Jesus did many other signs in the presence of His disciples, which are not written in this book; but these are written that you may believe that Jesus is the Christ, the Son of God, and that believing you may have life in His name." – John 20: 30-31 NKJV.

After Yeshua had spent 40 days with the disciples, post-resurrection, **"He commanded them not to depart from Jerusalem, but to wait for the Promise of the Father, "which," He said, "you have heard from Me; for John truly baptized with water, but you shall be baptized with the Holy Spirit not many days from now." Therefore, when they had come together, they asked Him, saying, "Lord, will You at this time restore the kingdom to Israel?" And He said to them, "It is not for you to know times or seasons which the Father has put in His own authority. But you shall receive power when the Holy Spirit has come upon you; and you shall be witnesses to Me in Jerusalem, and in all Judea and Samaria, and to the end of the earth."** – Acts 1: 4-8 NKJV.

He left them one final command and commissioned his disciples to **"Go therefore and make disciples of all the nations, baptizing them in the name of the Father and of the Son and of the Holy Spirit, teaching them to observe all things that I have commanded you; and lo, I am with you always, even to the end of the age."** – Matthew 28:19-20 NKJV.

Since He had restored all his disciples and followers and told them all that He needed to say, **"He was received up into Heaven, and sat down at the right hand of God." – Mark 16:19 NKJV.** The disciples immediately went out and began to minister to people, preaching to them the life of the Lord Jesus Christ and His works. Amen.

CHAPTER 3C

Holy Spirit

"If you love Me, keep My commandments. And I will pray the Father, and He will give you another Helper, that He may abide with you forever— the Spirit of truth, whom the world cannot receive, because it neither sees Him nor knows Him; but you know Him, for He dwells with you and will be in you. I will not leave you orphans; I will come to you. - John 14:15-18

Before it was time for Yeshua to uphold the cross and bear the sacrifice for the sins of many, He assured His disciples and for the sake of all those who would come to believe in Him; He would send the Holy Spirit as a Helper and the Leader into all truth. He specifically stated that those in the world (sinners) are not able to receive this Holy Sprit because the world does not know Yeshua intimately like believers do. Yeshua in this sense, can be seen as a Fatherly figure to His people because He does not leave people alone like orphans, rather He was sending the Holy Spirit, which is His Spirit, to guide all believers and believers to come into a fruitful relationship with the Father and Son whilst on the earth and to be a Helper in times of distress. The Holy Spirit is the one who facilitates God's presence in places where believers gather and convicts the hearts of non-believers to repent of sin. The Holy Spirit is the third person in the Blessed Trinity. He is also alive, like God and Yeshua, has His thoughts and feelings towards us. He mimics Yeshua in every way.

Yeshua started His ministry 2000+ years ago and His ministry is still ongoing, with the Holy Spirit spearheading His mission through the first disciples and believers all over the world in this present age. All believers have the right to receive the Holy Spirit when they come into faith with Yeshua. The Holy Spirit is a seal into the faith, when a person becomes a Christian. It is like a branding which determines the person belongs to someone or something. The Holy Spirit determines that a Christian belongs to God through Yeshua and to the Body of Christ here on earth. **"In Him you also trusted, after you heard the word of truth, the gospel of your salvation; in whom also, having believed, you were sealed with the Holy Spirit of promise..."** – **Ephesians 1:13 NKJV.** The scriptures goes on to add in Verse 14 that the Holy Spirit is **"the guarantee of our inheritance until the redemption of the purchased possession, to the praise of His glory."** When we carry the branding of Christ, we also carry the right to an inheritance shared in Christ Jesus in the next life. The Holy Spirit prepares us to work in this life and to enjoy His inheritance in eternal glory.

The Holy Spirit came upon His disciples, after his resurrection and ascent into heaven, in **Acts 2:1-4 NKJV-**

"When the day of Pentecost came, they were all together in one place. Suddenly a sound like the blowing of a violent wind came from heaven and filled the whole house where they were sitting. They saw what seemed to be tongues of fire that separated and came to rest on each of

them. All of them were filled with the Holy Spirit and began to speak in other tongues as the Spirit enabled them.

The people at Pentecost received power from the Holy Spirit and received Him personally into their Spirit for the first time. With this new discovered power, they began speaking in "tongues". Speaking in tongues is speaking in a heavenly language, one which the natural mind cannot understand or comprehend because this language transcends the understanding of this Earth. **"For if I pray in a tongue, my spirit prays, but my understanding is unfruitful." – 1 Corinthians 14:14 NKJV.**

Speaking in tongues is a powerful prayer weapon and tool which edifies us in our Spirit. **"He who speaks in a tongue edifies himself…" – 1 Corinthians 14:4 NKJV.** To edify ourselves means to build ourselves us up or construct ourselves further into Christlikeness. We sharpen our spiritual hearts and minds to become more like Christ and it helps us to develop a greater capacity to walk and act in righteousness.

When we speak in tongues, we speak directly to the Father in heaven as a prayer and the Holy Spirit prays through us for what we really need. We can also pray in tongues as a starting point to our prayer when we don't really know what to pray. We allow the Holy Spirit to take over our tongues. It is a guided prayer and it is much better to pray a prayer which is guided in holiness, than pray a prayer which can possibly be guided by selfish ambition or lustful desires. **"For he who speaks in a tongue does not speak to men but to God, for no one understands him; however, in the spirit he speaks mysteries." -1 Corinthians 14:2 NKJV.**

To walk in the fullness of the Holy Spirit means also to have access to the "Gifts of the Spirit". These gifts embody the nature, power and authority that Christ possessed and since we share in His inheritance, we also have every right to receive these gifts.

To receive the Gifts of the Spirit, we first ought to be filled with the Holy Spirit. We can do this by having mature Christians lay hands and pray for you or you can simply ask Yeshua for this baptism and prepare your heart and mind to receive from Him. On another note, a believer can also receive the Baptism of the Holy Spirit, which takes place in the Spirit and it activates a new level in your walk and communion with God to be a significantly more effective tool for His glory. This baptism boosts your daily walk in Him and helps you to effectively carry out His mission to bring to gospel to the world, make disciples of all nations and teach them to obey what Yeshua taught, ultimately bringing more souls to be saved. You do not necessarily need to receive the Baptism of the Holy Spirit to grow your giftings, but why not have an upgrade in the Spirit to work more effectively?

The gifts of the Spirit **"is given to each one for the profit of all: for to one is given the word of wisdom through the Spirit, to another the word of knowledge through the same Spirit, to another faith by the same Spirit, to another gifts of healings by the same Spirit, to another the working of miracles, to another prophecy, to another discerning of spirits, to another different kinds of tongues, to another the interpretation of tongues. But one and the same Spirit works all these things,**

distributing to each one individually as He wills." – 1 Corinthians 12: 7-11.

These gifts are meant to bless, encourage and comfort other people because your life is a service to others. Yeshua left the prime example of being a servant and He expects us to serve one another. These gifts can also be described as having a special anointing(s) or abilities to minister to other people up to the full measure of the effectiveness and the power of the Holy Spirit. These gifts are freely given by the Holy Spirit and it measures the amount of connection a believer has with the Holy Spirit. These gifts can grow within you, but not by your own accord, because they only come from and are developed by the power of the Holy Spirit.

It is really important to understand your gifts, if you come into faith with Yeshua. Every believer, as long as they have the Holy Spirit, has giftings within them. A lot of people operate in their giftings without even knowing them. For example, I used to start hearing from God when I was 18. As I continued to hear for myself over the years, I began hearing words of knowledge for others, but I did not know this was a gift. Then, in the recent time, I began to operate prophetically, whilst still being ignorant of the gifts and not have a sound understanding of them. Only this year, 2023, in the month of April, did I realize I had been operating in two gifts.

Since I know all the gifts and have a sound understanding of them, I am able to operate more effectively and pursue the Lord to develop and potentially receive more of the giftings. Knowing and identifying your personal spiritual gifts give you a sense of direction as to what the Lord has called you to do in life. You begin to develop a stronger sense of direction and are able to channel your focus towards His walk, rather than going off into the world and figuring out what you're meant to be doing.

We need to have an equal respect for all the giftings and not underate other gifts. This is because God designed every person to have a different experience of gifts in Him and they are all meant to work together because they come from the one same Holy Spirit.

Let's break down the gifts of the Spirit-

1. The *word(s) of wisdom* is a gift which enables a person to have specific discovery surrounding biblical truths, and enables that person to apply these truths to their life. Operating in wisdom can help a person make appropriate choices and save them from unnecessary troubles, propelling the person to carefully base their life on the direction and truths of the Scriptures. Wisdom comes freely from God and everyone needs wisdom to live an abundant life.

2. The *word(s) of knowledge* comes from a personal revelation from God. This gift is closely related to the *words of wisdom*. It can come hand in hand with it as well. The *word(s) of knowledge* allows a person to understand the deeper mysteries of the Word of God and circumstances in their life or other people's lives. This revelation, is imparted by the Holy Spirit and gives the receiver supernatural knowledge about a subject or another person, which helps to edify the person receiving the word and other people. The *word(s) of knowledge* are often used to reveal Jesus to unbelievers, by revealing something specific about the person, through the Holy Spirit. The revelation could be present or past circumstances, which the giver themselves could not know without the Holy Spirit and this gift!

3. *Faith*, as we know comes by hearing and seeing the wonders of God. However, there are certain circumstances where we need a new level of faith to dare to believe God for the most impossible

or unlikely results. This faith propels a person to take that leap of faith to believe God for even greater things. A deeper capacity of faith causes God to move in a higher level; therefore, achieving extraordinary results for that person and others involved. It is a gift that every believer needs, because **"without faith it is impossible to please Him, for he who comes to God must believe that He is, and that He is a rewarder of those who diligently seek Him"- Hebrews 11:6 NKJV.**

4. *Gifts of healing* allows the person to operate the healing power of God in and through themselves. They receive the healing anointing, whereby having the accompanied faith, they lay hands on the sick and cause them to recover. This gift carries the supernatural healing presence of God and can also be used in deliverance to cast out demons. This gift anoints the user to lay hands on another to align the sick person's body, soul and spirit to the will of God.

5. *Working of miracles* is a gift that operates in the supernatural and defies the natural order of things. This gift involves fasting, prayer or obedience to be used, and once operated in the Spirit, can achieve extraordinary supernatural results in a near to impossible manner. A person who operates in this gift often displays the miracles, signs and wonders that Yeshua displayed.

6. *Prophecy* is my personal favourite. This gift requires full submission to God and trustworthiness in His eyes because operating in this gift means to be the mouthpiece of the voice of God here on earth. It does not come from the believer's own wisdom or understanding but comes from the Holy Spirit's words and prompting only. Speaking prophetic words is a big responsibility in the Body and this gift is used to exhort, edify, give direction and comfort

other believers. The gift of prophecy can help believers understand their call and their future purposes.

7. *Discerning of spirits* helps a believer to understand the supernatural source of messages or activities and helps to give them clarity as to whether it is from God, the world, of man's own heart or from the devil. It can be described as a supernatural detection system which helps believers to understand root causes of situations or ailments.

8. *Different kinds of tongues* help a believer to speak in different types of heavenly languages. Praying in and developing this gift helps a person to have a stronger prayer life and increases intimacy with God. It also increases edification as God gives the person more tongues in which to speak.

9. *Interpretation of tongues* is a gift that helps a person to receive divine translation or interpretation of a message received in tongues. In congregations where the Spirit of God is moving, one person may be touched to release a word in tongues and no human mind can understand or interpret. The one with this gift has the advantage to understand the word given in tongues, and can then translate it for the congregation in a human language so that everyone can understand what is spoken from Heaven and be edified in unity. Having this gift also helps the believer to understand the mind of God.

Every believer should desire to have all or as many gifts as possible so that we can all lead full and abundant lives like Yeshua did on this Earth. This is because He possessed all these gifts and since He wants us to become like Him, we should endeavour to desire, pray for and grow in these gifts by the leading of the Holy Spirit. These gifts can be given to us by the

Holy Spirit in time, as it takes a deeper walk to develop more and harbor more of God. Always seek the Lord and ask Him directly if you wish to receive more and let Him plant these gifts in you, according to His will.

We have to remember that when practicing these gifts, they need to come from love. Love for the Body of Christ and non-believers needs to be the significant driver for us when operating these gifts because without love, it is fruitless. God operates on the basis of love and His entire plan of salvation derived from His love for the human race to begin with.

All in all, everything we are called to do in this world comes first from the Lord. We need to humble ourselves and remember that we do His works not just by our strength, but by the prompting and the leading of the Holy Spirit. Yeshua very carefully taught **"I am the vine; you are the branches. He who abides in Me, and I in him, bears much fruit; for without Me you can do nothing." – John 15:5 NKJV.** We abide in Christ and vice versa through the Holy Spirt and we ought to heed the voice and the prompting of His Spirit because we need direction at every stage in our lives. We need to carefully discern and examine the voices which we hear. We, as believers, will know His voice and we must follow Him.

It took me many years, after I became a Christian, to learn to follow His voice properly. I was always going off and pursuing my own dreams and ambitions and was constantly grieving the Holy Spirit. If you do this, you can end up on the wrong paths or even be led to destruction because the enemy is always looking for the Christians who are going off course to trap them and cause them to stumble. This can also lead to backsliding, which I have done quite a few times. We need the Holy Spirit more than we think and it is a daily reliance upon Him. I wish I could take back all the years that I did not heed His voice but I have learnt my lessons the hard way. The Holy Spirit can be grieved when we go our own way, or walk in disobedience, so please do not grieve Him. My prayer is for you, as you read all of this, is that you would discipline yourself right now and train your ears to hear His voice and train your heart and inner man to obey and be led by His prompting.

All in all, we must always remember that **"Jesus Christ is the same yesterday, today, and forever." – Hebrews 13:8 NKJV.** Your inheritance awaits you.

CHAPTER 4
The Five-Fold Ministry

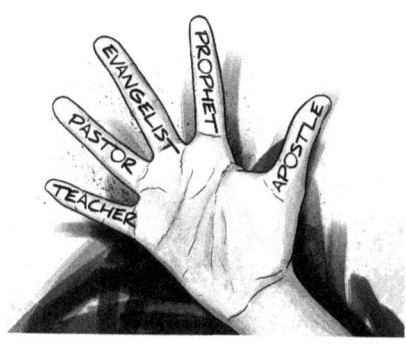

"And He Himself gave some to be apostles, some prophets, some evangelists, and some pastors and teachers, for the equipping of the saints for the work of ministry, for the edifying of the body of Christ, till we all come to the unity of the faith and of the knowledge of the Son of God, to a perfect man, to the measure of the stature of the fullness of Christ; that we should no longer be children, tossed to and fro and carried about with every wind of doctrine, by the trickery of men, in the cunning craftiness of deceitful plotting, but, speaking the truth in love, may grow up in all things into Him who is the head—Christ— from whom the whole body, joined and knit together by what every joint supplies, according to the effective working by which every part does its share, causes growth of the body for the edifying of itself in love." - Ephesians 4:11 NKJV

Yeshua is the Head of the Body of Christ, as we know. Under Him are the five categories that believers are called to. These are apostles, prophets, evangelists, pastors and teachers. These areas were set up by God for the purpose of equipping His Church for the work of ministry. The ministry should stand on the basis of the Great Commission which Yeshua left for His disciples before He ascended to the right hand of the Father. He said **"Go therefore and make disciples of all the nations, baptizing them in the name of the Father and of the Son and of the Holy Spirit, teaching them to observe all things that I have commanded you; and lo, I am with you always, even to the end of the age." – Matthew 28:19-20 NKJV.** This foundation is key to serving Yeshua because this was His overall and is still His overall mission- to win souls for the Kingdom so that each created person may know God, be reunited with God and make it into His glorious Kingdom.

The five-fold ministry was established to edify the body of Christ and all believers. Each pillar of the ministry edifies the body in its own unique way. The edification process involves building up faith and knowledge in the believers, bringing them closer together so that all may have the same heavenly goal and the supports each believer needs, to develop the full potential in their calling in Christ Jesus. Edification is very important because Yeshua called us to serve the body as well. As each person is built up in their faith, they get to experience the glory and power of God in a higher realm and gain more revelation. This leads to them walking according to their call and not being pulled away by the world, so that they can become a sharper tool in their service to God and to the Body.

The Body is called to be sanctified continuously in their walk, so that all believers may strive to become like Yeshua's perfect nature on this earth. Although believers will never fully become perfect until we are in the

Kingdom, the standard has been set for believers to try their best to mimic Yeshua and live their lives like He did. Becoming like Christ requires believers to grow continuously into maturity. This is because the next generation of born-again Christians need mentorship, therefore, there will always be a need for a Christian mentor. Not only is it pleasing to God to walk in Christ's full measure, but the actions of reflecting the nature of Christ in a believer's walk will speak to those who are non-believers, therefore, convicting them to live a fulfilled and abundant life under the Shadow of the Almighty.

Having one Body come together and believing in one faith supports Biblical doctrine more effectively. This fallen world carries many false doctrines on receiving salvation, but if the Body of Christ can walk strongly in Biblical doctrine and reflect the good conduct of Christ's love and nature, it would be more convincing for the worldly doctrines to appear misleading. A doctrine which is upheld by Yeshua and cooperatively engaged with by a strong Body can lead to a greater measure of lost souls coming to the Kingdom. There is a need for the truth to be spoken in love because the world is defensive and resentful of the truth, being caught up in the devil's web of lies. Love is the way to win souls for the Kingdom, and all doctrine should be measured out with Christlike works and love.

Each member of the Body is expected to contribute to the rest of the Body so that all members are built up and not lacking anything. With joint resources and joint cooperation, the message of the Gospel will be more convincing to the rest of the world. We as members, are called to be examples and if the enemy sees any contradictions, he will pounce on those contradictions, blow it up with lies and use it to accuse the brethren. To some of the non-believers in which the enemy works in, it would be a good opportunity to for them to highlight contradictions, blow up any failures to make it look worse than it is, and spread false lies about the gospel message. The unity of the Body of Christ is necessary, which is why love must be at the forefront of the mind of all believers.

The enemy constantly seeks to isolate members of the Body of Christ so that He can steal the seeds of the gospel planted in them, kill their faith in Yeshua and destroy their livelihoods, using temptations to engage the strayed believer with. It is very important to be connected to local church or homegroup where Spirit-filled believers are gathered.

The Body of Christ may be filled with people of different races, backgrounds or environments, but in Yeshua's eyes, we are all one cohort of the Bride of Christ.

"And let us consider one another in order to stir up love and good works, not forsaking the assembling of ourselves together, as is the manner of some, but exhorting one another, and so much the more as you see the Day approaching." – Hebrews 10:24-25 NKJV.

1. *Apostles* mean "one who is sent on mission". The first apostles were the first 12 disciples that Yeshua chose to follow Him on His ministry. **"One of those days Jesus went out to a mountainside to pray, and spent the night praying to God. When morning came, he called his disciples to him and chose twelve of them, whom he also designated apostles: Simon (whom he named Peter), his brother Andrew, James, John, Philip, Bartholomew, Matthew, Thomas, James son of Alphaeus, Simon who was called the Zealot, Judas son of James, and Judas Iscariot, who became a traitor." – Luke 6:12-16 NKJV.** These people were part of the first pillar of the five-fold ministry, before the fivefold ministry was officially established. They followed Yeshua wherever He went and

were taught by Him to teach others what they were taught and to perform signs, wonders and miracles in His Name.

In today's world, apostles are official representatives of the Body of Christ charged with the mission of bringing the gospel to their local areas or nations. They are often people who are "sent" somewhere, charged with delivering the gospel of truth. Apostles usually have an inward sense of God's call to go to a certain area, have a sense that they need to undertake a specific mission for the gospel purpose and can also become burdened for it. Apostles carry the focus of the kingdom within themselves. They endeavor to introduce the gospel of Yeshua to communities, with the intention to set up a kingdom community. They pioneer churches or a new movement of God in new areas to facilitate the growth of new believers in specific communities and to win more souls.

Apostles carry the authority of the kingdom because they are literally charged to bring Heaven to their target audience or communities. Within a church, apostles look to accumulate resources to go out on mission trips, they train and develop missionaries, have to focus of kingdom impact to their target audience or communities, strengthen the foundations of the gospel and even father leaders in the church. An example of an apostle is someone who brings the gospel, with a group, to a village in South America and begins to establish the foundation of the gospel message to the local people. They preach the gospel and cater to their needs however they can, displaying an example of the Kingdom purposes.

2. *Prophets* are the mouthpieces of God, declaring His will over a local area, town or nation. In the Old Testament, Isaiah was regarded as the first major prophet. Isaiah was caught up into Heaven into the presence of God and God ordained Him to be a prophet. God cleaned the mouth of Isaiah, rendering him worthy to be his mouthpiece in **Isaiah 6: 6-7 NKJV- "Then one of the seraphim flew to me, having in his hand a live coal which he had taken with the tongs from the altar. And he touched my mouth with it, and said: "Behold, this has touched your lips; Your iniquity is taken away, and your sin purged."**

Isaiah 6: 8-9 NKJV continues to show us that Isaiah offered himself to be used by God and God gave him the words to speak- **"Also I heard the voice of the Lord, saying: "Whom shall I send; And who will go for Us?" Then I said, "Here *am* I! Send me." And He said, "Go, and tell this people: 'Keep on hearing, but do not understand. Keep on seeing, but do not perceive.'"**

In today's world, a Prophet of God is one who is still a mouthpiece of God and one who declares the will of God to their local congregation, community or nations. Their main purpose in the Body of Christ is to edify, exhort and comfort others, through what God is saying for them. They are burdened to speak what the Holy Spirit gives them from God, which could be warnings, telling of what is to come in the future and primarily, what God wants to say at the present time. Within the scriptures, there were 48 prophets mentioned who were spread out in the Old and New Testament. These prophets experienced a very close and intimate relationship with God, like a friendship, and therefore God would reveal the mysteries and the secrets of the Kingdom to these people. These people would then be instructed by the Spirit of God, or God Himself to go to places and declare what God wants to do in the target area or bring the warning of God to areas of wicked practises and be called to repent, lest they were judged.

There are different distinct ways that prophets receive messages from God. These include: knowing, seeing, hearing and feeling. Knowing is to receive supernatural knowledge about a subject. Seeing is to have the "seer" anointing and be able to see visions or receive dreams pertaining to specific subjects. Hearing is to hear the Voice of God within the inner spirit of the prophet and then receive instructions to share what they have heard. Feeling is to have a supernatural gut instinct about certain decisions or places. Since prophets have been given authority with their speaking, they have supernatural capabilities to speak to bodies of government with authority, speak in a manner that commands respect and even speak to the environment to establish a heavenly environment.

3. *Evangelists* are preachers in their own right, who are burdened for and find Godly joy in bringing the good news of the Gospel to others. Evangelism can range from many forms and many areas,

from having a private conversation with a friend and telling them about the Good News or standing in front of a crowd in a shopping center and calling people to repentance. They proclaim the Good News in response to the call of the Great Commission and bring glad tidings. They are also known as messengers because they carry the message of Yeshua to the unsaved. It is good to note that, in a sense, every believer is called to evangelise to others. Even talking to your next-door neighbor over the fence is considered evangelism. **"Walk in wisdom toward those who are outside, redeeming the time. Let your speech always be with grace, seasoned with salt, that you may know how you ought to answer each one." Colossians 4:5-6 NKJV.**

4. *Pastors* are called to one specific church to "shepherd" and edify the flock of believers which have been assigned under them. The name of pastor means "shepherd". They are called and trained to model the "Chief Shepherd", who is Yeshua. With their position of leadership in the church, their role in the Body of Christ involves leading their weekly church services 2 or 3 times a week, providing counsel based on sound doctrine to people in their congregation who need spiritual guidance or help, they visit believers in their homes or in hospitals, they study the Word of God thoroughly because they are required to preach sound doctrine on different topics in the Bible and attend to business within the church amongst other leaders. Pastors have a very big responsibility because they are responsible for the messages they give out, which can very easily influence a lot of believers. If an incorrect message is being preached to believers who lack discernment, then the pastor is also held responsible by God for leading believers astray.

5. *Teachers* are trainers and instructors in the matters of the Word of God. They also are required to study the Word of God to provide teaching on sound doctrine. Teachers can disciple believers in a one-on-one setting, or like a school setting. Teachers contribute to the Body of Christ by literally teaching on the Word of God in Bible colleges, churches or external locations where faith seminars are being conducted. Teachers look to equip their students with the correct tools and knowledge to contribute to the Body of Christ; to bring about illumination, revelation and transformation concerning the Word of God and the call of God over people's lives.

Each person in the body of Christ has a special role towards the Body of Christ because **"we are His workmanship, created in Christ Jesus for good works, which God prepared beforehand that we should walk in them" – Ephesians 2:10 NKJV.** Discovering our roles in the Body requires us to seek the Lord with everything we have in us, and He, in His perfect time, will reveal the paths we need to take. He wants us to first develop our relationship with Him in a close and intimate manner. He will then open doors and make it clear to us where he wants us to contribute and in which office or pillar of the five-fold ministry we belong to. We cannot do anything apart from Christ so we need to seek Him first above anything else. **"But seek first the kingdom of God and His righteousness, and all these things shall be added to you." – Matthew 6:33 NKJV.**

My prayer for you is that the Lord will lead you to discovering your purpose as you continually press forward to see His face. Do not be discouraged if you do not see results immediately but continue to trust in Him and He will make your path straight. There is always a season for everything and you can be sure your season of discovering your calling will come to pass, in His time.

PRAYER POINT

Father in Heaven. I call to You in the name of Jesus Christ and I ask that You help me to discover the path You want me to take. Please establish my foot on a high place and show me the glorious paths of righteousness which You want me to walk in. Lord, I know You have called me for such a time as this, and I ask that You establish me strongly in what You want me to do. I look to discover Your will alone for my life.

I thank You Lord that You have given me abundant life. I thank You that You will reveal all things to me as I develop my walk and intimacy with You first. Help me to serve the Body of Christ and I commit myself willingly to the Office of Your choosing.

In Jesus Christ's name, Amen.

CHAPTER 5

The Power of His Word

I want to first acknowledge that God's Word, in the Bible, is the only Word that is actually alive and active in this fallen world. His Word is the ultimate authority over everything which exists. Anything which contradicts the Word of God is false. **"For the word of God is living and powerful, and sharper than any two-edged sword, piercing even to the division of soul and spirit, and of joints and marrow, and is a discerner of the thoughts and intents of the heart." – Hebrews 4:12 NKJV.** His Living Word penetrates anything and anyone. It is actively working in line with the will of God. For whatever God wills, He speaks and it comes to pass in His time. His Word has authority over anything and everything ever created.

2 Timothy 3:16 NKJV says **"All Scripture *is* given by inspiration of God, and *is* profitable for doctrine, for reproof, for correction, for instruction in righteousness, that the man of God may be complete, thoroughly equipped for every good work."** This gives us the foundation of faith that every single word written in the Scriptures came from God alone. We need to base our life and align our personal will according to what the Word of God teaches, instructs and speaks. If you want to live free from the bondages and clutches of sin and death, you need to feed on His Word everyday as much as you can.

We can experience the life in His Word if we consume His Word daily and watch as it changes the way we think, and therefore the way we live. Our own ideas and will are slowly put aside because as we read, we begin to adopt His ideas and His will on how to live a very fulfilled life. There is so much clarity in reading the Scriptures and it provides directions. It is the best "how to" manual for living life in this world.

His Word creates.

God's spoken word is filled with creative energy and life. He created everything seen and unseen. From the very beginning of time, we can see that God literally spoke the words which brought every living thing into existence. Keep in mind that God spoke life into existence, therefore, everything created is actually living. God literally **said, "Let there be light"; and there was light."- Genesis 1:3 NKJV**, and he continued to say "Let there be" throughout the beginning of Genesis until all the Heavens and the earth, the living things, the sky, day and night and everything we can see in nature, were created and formed. God created the multiplication effect in animals and humans by saying **"Be fruitful and multiply…" – Genesis 1: 22 NKJV.** If He did not speak it, it would not happen nor would it exist. His creative words which spoke the universe into existence holds everything created in place. This can be seen because everything still exists. If God were to speak for everything to be erased, everything seen and unseen would be gone in a snap.

His Word heals.

The Word of God can bring healing and restoration to the most corrupt minds, spirits and bodies. His words bring life, and the byproduct of the life He speaks brings healing and restoration. His Word offers us a remedy and medicine for the different kinds of pain and hardships we may experience. When you meditate on His Word, and as you personalize the verses of Scripture, what happens is that a spiritual seed is planted in your Spirit. As you continue to develop yourself in the Lord, the seed begins to grow and produce physical healing to your mind and body.

I witnessed a miracle in this area when I was reading Psalm 91 to a boy who had severe paranoia and anxiety for his safety. As I ministered to this boy and offered Him the comfort of Psalm 91, his fears immediately dissipated because he was supernaturally convinced that he was being protected by God. I have never seen dreadful anxiety converted to pure joy in a couple of minutes, as a result of the truth of the word of His protection. There are times I have experienced immense joy when I had been feeling down, just by repeating Psalms or Scriptures to myself and I supernaturally have my joy restored.

His Word instructs and reproofs.

The Word of God gives us a doctrine which comes from God. This doctrine instructs and teaches us how to live a righteous life which is pleasing to God and brings about the abundant nature of God into our daily experiences. To obey His doctrine provides an understanding and deeper clarity into the nature of God, the rewards of following Him, His personal relationship with us believers and helps us to keep a good moral conduct in life.

His instructions are not to make our life hard, but rather to place boundaries over us so we do not step into zones that can get us hurt. If God says do not commit adultery, and you disobey, you can find yourself in trouble in the form of physical, mental or spiritual anguish. This is because, you did not obey His Word but chose to entertain the sin which comes from demons. Like it or not, there is a price to pay if you disobey Him and do not repent. His Word instructs that we all need to be redeemed to become righteous.

His Word instructs repentance and continuously rebukes sinners so that they might recognize the reality of their standing with God. His Word tells us that **"friendship with the world is enmity with God? Whoever therefore wants to be a friend of the world makes himself an enemy of God." – James 4:4 NKJV.** When His Word rebukes sinners, it does so with a conviction to turn sinners to the truth. People need to understand the reality of their standing with God, so that they can escape the bondages of sin and its influence over their life! His instructions extinguish the pride of life so that no man can ever say they have figured out how to live a "good" life. If they did not follow the doctrine of His Word, then it is all vanity and not pleasing to God.

His Word instructs us to turn to Yeshua for the forgiveness of sins and life everlasting. This is because He has revealed to us in the Scriptures that Yeshua is the only way to be righteous in the sight of God. Whenever a believer needs to provide correction to someone who is going astray, they need to do so on the basis of what the Word of God says and use the Scriptures to instruct the one who has strayed away back onto the paths of righteousness. His instructions are there for us to use to minister to those who might be harboring contradictory doctrines.

His Word saves us.

Yeshua was God manifest in the flesh and He was also the Word of God come down in the flesh. **John1:1 NKJV** says **"In the beginning was the Word, and the Word was with God, and the Word was God."** and it later goes on to say in **verse 14 "And the Word became flesh and dwelt among us, and we beheld His glory, the glory as of the only begotten of the Father, full of grace and truth.** God and His Word are one, and at this point in time, the Word of God incarnated into the world as Yeshua. Whatsoever He taught and spoke, He spoke with the same authority that God had when He created all things into existence.

The Word of God was given to us in a written form and in a human form of Yeshua to ultimately save us and bring us to salvation. When Yeshua spoke to people, He was able to convict them so thoroughly in their hearts that they knew He was the Son of God. One of His closest disciples, Peter, said with full conviction **"Lord, to whom shall we go? You have the words of eternal life." – John 6:68 NKJV.** Yeshua came to also to fulfill the Mosaic law of the Old Testament and He did so in His perfect life. Everything He spoke about was pertaining to what God wanted to speak to humanity, including that which He already spoke in the Old Testament, therefore supporting the notion that Yeshua was the living and breathing Word of God who had come to speak of and bring salvation.

If we obey the Word of God in trusting Yeshua for our salvation and redemption, then we experience the result of His Word saving us.

My salvation story came as a result of experiencing the power of the Word of God. I was 15 years old and I was invited to church for the first time. I had been experiencing feelings of emptiness and I was looking for meaning to my life. I came and met someone who gave me a pocket size copy of the Gideon's Gospel of John. I helped myself to the entire book, carefully analyzing all the written words of Yeshua in red, trying to understand who Yeshua was and what He did. That small pocket size Scripture gave me the faith I needed and conviction in my heart to bow to the Lordship of Yeshua. I did not need a reason to believe in the Son of God. I only know that what I read was true, as I read it, and my heart became convicted. This shows me that the Word of God was working on my heart to believe in Him, not on my mind. There was no cognitive reasoning involved for me to question WHY I should believe, because my heart said "Believe"

CHAPTER 6

God's Protection

Psalm 91 NKJV -

"He who dwells in the secret place of the Most High
Shall abide under the shadow of the Almighty.
I will say of the Lord, "He is my refuge and my fortress;
My God, in Him I will trust.""

The Psalmist describes the presence of God as His protective place. The secret place of God is being hidden away in His Presence, where there is no darkness and where nothing can hurt you. His shadow covers you in your daily walk with Him, therefore nothing will touch You. When they look at you, they see the shadow of God over you, where God is next to you. The presence of the Lord God is a place where you are defended on all corners, like a fortress. There are high walls all around you. The psalmist knows in his heart that only the Lord is the one who protects, and is able to build trust in Him for that reason. You can trust the Lord to protect you in all your paths.

**"Surely, He shall deliver you from the snare of the fowler
And from the perilous pestilence.
He shall cover you with His feathers,
And under His wings you shall take refuge;**

The Lord will work to set you free from any traps that catch you off guard. When you are caught in a trap prepared by the enemy, call to Him and He will set you free from it. We are called to walk freely in His Presence. Pestilence comes in the form of sickness and diseases. Any pandemic which shakes the world of unbelievers, has no place in the believers' lives because the promise of His protection is there. You will take refuge as He covers you with His arms. The might of the Lord can withstand any evil projectile. Find your place under Him, not in the false safety of the world.

**His truth shall be your shield and buckler.
You shall not be afraid of the terror by night,
Nor of the arrow that flies by day,
Nor of the pestilence that walks in darkness,
Nor of the destruction that lays waste at noonday."**

His truth, being the truth of His Word, if you follow it, shall protect you. If you walk in His ways, you are walking righteously and the righteous are always kept. His Word shall be your personal shield, which shields you from the evil influences experienced in this life. You will be brave and courageous because you trust in Him. You will face terrors of the night, arrows and projectiles from the enemy that come during the day, the diseases and sicknesses during the night and the destruction you see in the world around you during the day, but you will NOT be moved. You will see and be protected because it will not destroy you, as you remain in Him.

A thousand may fall at your side,
And ten thousand at your right hand;
But it shall not come near you.
Only with your eyes shall you look,
And see the reward of the wicked.

As you see the people around you affected by calamities and disasters in their personal world or in the world itself, you will not be touched. You will be supernaturally guarded. What the enemy sent for your destruction, will be rebounded off you because His presence blocks you. You will see and observe the destruction that comes to the wicked. The arrows they sent to you, will be sent back to them. The words of destruction they speak to you (for example- witchcraft), will be sent back to them and they will fall into their own traps.

Because you have made the Lord, who is my refuge,
Even the Most High, your dwelling place,
No evil shall befall you,
Nor shall any plague come near your dwelling;

The only reason you are protected is because you chose to make the Lord God your constant place of dwelling. Protection comes as you continuously turn to Him, separate yourself from the world and choose to abide in His presence every day. As a result, no evil shall affect you and there will be no darkness or disease coming to your home. He guards your home all day and all night.

For He shall give His angels charge over you,
To keep you in all your ways.
In their hands they shall bear you up,
Lest you dash your foot against a stone.

He will command warring and guardian angels to stand by your side to protect you in the unseen realms. He will instruct them to watch over your comings and goings and to make sure you are untouched by the darkness. If any demon attempts to come near you, His angels will fight them off and remind them to Whom you belong to. His angels will lift you up and ensure you do not stumble in your daily path.

You shall tread upon the lion and the cobra,
The young lion and the serpent you shall trample underfoot.

Yeshua said we have authority to trample over the enemy. As we remain in Him and His protection, we have the freedom to step over the plans of the enemy and rebuke them. We have an inheritance of protection and safety in the Kingdom. We ought to walk in our authority, that Yeshua gave to us and establish our comings and goings with boldness in His Name.

"Because he has set his love upon Me, therefore I will deliver him;
I will set him on high, because he has known My name.
He shall call upon Me, and I will answer him;
I will be with him in trouble;
I will deliver him and honor him.
With long life I will satisfy him,
And show him My salvation."

The Lord God will observe your love for him and will honor your love by delivering you from the darkness and any plans of the wicked. He will lift you up and set you on a high place because you intimately know His name. Whenever you call on God, He will answer because He hears you quickly. He promises never to leave us nor forsake us and to continuously be by our side. The Lord promises to deliver us many times over as He has repeated and will honor your faithfulness to Him. He will give you eternal life if your faith is in His Son Yeshua and will reveal the glory of the Kingdom to you, now and forever.

Amen.

The Armor of God.

Ephesians 6:11-17 NKJV-

"Put on the whole armor of God, that you may be able to stand against the wiles of the devil. For we do not wrestle against flesh and blood, but against principalities, against powers, against the rulers of the darkness of this age, against spiritual hosts of wickedness in the heavenly places.

When we enter into the ranks of the Kingdom of Heaven, in this life, we also enter into a battlefield. The battle of light against the darkness, which originated since the enemy, the devil, was cast out of heaven along with one-third of the angels. Since then, the devil and his angels have been waging warfare against God. Since they cannot actually touch God, they redirect their attacks against the beings who were created in His image, US! The enemy is very tactical and legalistic, willing to infiltrate the leaders of mankind to persuade them to adopt demonic methods of ruling over humans, and therefore causing great destruction.

There are numerous other tactics that the enemy has been using for the longest amount of time, however, one thing we must understand is this warfare is not a physical one but a spiritual one. The enemy used to have the upper hand on this earth until Yeshua came and won the victory for us. The only way you could lose the battle now is if you are ignorant to wiles of the devil, such as non-believers are, or if you willingly give in to evil temptation and give the enemy legal ground to establish his strongholds in your life.

Therefore, take up the whole armor of God, that you may be able to withstand in the evil day, and having done all, to stand.

We are blessed because we already have the victory to win the entire war, which will be won at the conclusion of the end times, however, the enemy still thinks he can win and will constantly be roaming around. looking for weak links in the Body of Christ to destroy. The Bible instructs us to resist him and remain protected by donning the whole armor of God so that we can withstand and continue to withstand the enemy, till our redemption comes.

Stand therefore, having girded your waist with truth, having put on the breastplate of righteousness, and having shod your feet with the preparation of the gospel of peace; above all, taking the shield of faith with which, you will be able to quench all the fiery darts of the wicked one. And take the helmet of salvation, and the sword of the Spirit, which is the word of God…"

You must wear the armor of God daily because the enemy will not stop. Make it a habit every morning, through prayer to wear the armor of God each morning, so you can be confident and ready to take on the day ahead. Stand firm and put on the following pieces of armor:

The belt of truth / girded with truth.

The belt is what holds the armor together. This truth is found in the Word of God and in the Lord Jesus Christ. You must equip yourself with truth by reading, meditating and praying the scriptures. We must have a firm understanding of the Word of God, with daily discipline so we can do what the Word says and be blessed. The truth also reminds us who we are and our identity. Too often, Christians get attacked because they lack the understanding or knowledge of who they are in Christ. You have to fill yourself with the knowledge of what Yeshua sees you as presently, and who He has called you to be. If you are a Christian- you are a son / daughter of the living God! You have a royal inheritance awaiting you in your eternal home – Heaven! You walk in the victory of Yeshua and you truly have the upper hand! This truth protects us from the lies of the world and the temptations of the flesh, which will result in destruction and death. The Word of God is the ultimate truth and the final authority.

The breastplate of righteousness.

The Scripture states that the Christian stands in **"the righteousness of God, through faith in Jesus Christ, to all and on all who believe." – Romans 3:22 NKJV.** We ought to don the breastplate of righteousness daily, because since we stand righteous in Him, His righteousness protects and guards our hearts from the quick and unexpected advances of the flesh. When temptation creeps in swiftly, our breastplate is able to protect our heart from deceit. The righteousness given to us causes us to check that our heart is walking with God rather than allowing it to pursue the desires of the world and evil. As you don His righteousness, practice the good works of the gospel and obey what He has commanded us, i.e. – caring for the sick, preaching and giving to the homeless, etc. We also need to understand that human righteousness is very imperfect and can bring a sense of pride. We need to humbly walk in that which He gave us, because our righteous identity comes from Yeshua alone. It was never ours to begin with. Our sin, for His righteousness.

Sandals of the gospel of peace / shod your feet with the gospel of peace.

When we stand on the truth of the gospel of peace, we stand on a firm foundation. In our daily walks, we need to walk in the firm foundation of the gospel, which brings life and peace to us and those around us. As we walk, we also need to act out the gospel message, i.e. – forgiving others, loving the unlovable, bearing others' burdens, etc. Knowing that we have peace in the gospel message- which is what Yeshua did for us, bring the gospel to the non-believers around you, always being ready to share the message with love and meekness. Pray to the Father to bring you down the paths of those whose hearts are being prepared to hear the gospel, then go boldly in faith, looking out for the ones whom the Holy Spirit highlights to you. The gospel message is something people cannot afford to miss out on. It will literally cost them their soul.

Shield of faith.

Often times, when you are running the race in the right direction, you will face attempts from the enemy to slow you down. When we go to battle to face the enemy, we need to guard ourselves and we automatically rely on our shield to block the arrows or the strikes of the enemy. The shield of faith is an effective tool to block demonic influences or hostile attacks. It is our primary defense weapon used in warfare. Our shield comes in the form of our faith in the Father. The greater our faith is, the greater the coverage of our shield. We ought to constantly be trusting only in God's power and protection during warfare so that we can remain steadfast and strongly rooted in all circumstances. Our Good Father works all attacks of evil for our good because He loves us and promises to protect us. Therefore, stand firm with your shield lifted to withstand the arrows of the enemy and watch as the hand of God destroys the opposing forces coming against you. Did you know that Roman soldiers used to band their shields together, forming a strong barricade. Find other believers who will hold their shield with yours and form a strong holy barricade. Your faith in the Lord will cause the barricade to withstand any amount of arrows or strikes.

Helmet of salvation.

A blow to the head would prove to be fatal. That is where our mind is. Everything we do and how we live our life comes from the way we think and perceive the world. Our mind is susceptible to receiving truths and lies. We have the capability to imagine thoughts which exalt themselves against the Lordship of Jesus Christ. An idle mind is the devil's playground. Our thoughts are constantly infiltrated by the enemy's doubts, deceit and evil. We have to carefully guard our mind. The helmet of salvation is our most crucial piece of armor. We ought to have the mind of Christ. Implanting the hope of salvation and redemption in our mind gives us the upper hand in every single battle we could ever face. We know what we have in the next life and the house of God is being prepared for us to enter. When you don the helmet of salvation, you are standing on the firm knowledge that Yeshua has already purchased salvation for you and not even the sting of death can defeat you. You must also guard what your mind entertains. To combat the battle of the mind, you need to feed your mind with Biblical truths and doctrines to counteract the lies of the enemy. As you have the hope of salvation imprinted into your head, you will always have the victory over any battle.

Sword of the Spirit.

Our sword is our only offensive weapon. The devil will strike, but we must learn to strike back harder utilizing the Word of God and our known authority in Yeshua which makes demons tremble. The more skilled you are with your sword, the deadlier your strikes become. You need to memorize scripture, which the Holy Spirit will bring back to your memory and use those scriptures to combat the lies of the enemy. When Yeshua was tempted, He remembered and quoted scripture, as can be seen in **Matthew 4:3-2 NKJV "the tempter came to him and said, "If you are the Son of God, tell these stones to become bread."** Jesus answered, "It is written: 'Man shall not live on bread alone, but on every word that comes from the mouth of God.'".

Continue to sharpen your blade by arming yourself with more and more scripture passages. Continue to commit them to active memory and verbalize them as much as you can in your daily walk. Always remember the example Yeshua used. The key words are "It is written". You need to remind the enemy that the scriptures you quote are written in the Word of God. The enemy knows very well that the Word of God is the final authority over everything, even over him and his minions.

According to the scriptures, it is written, that we are world overcomers and **"more than conquerors through Him who loved us." – Romans 8:37 NKJV.** So, don your armor daily, anticipate the plans and tactics of the enemy. Ensure there are no open doors (unconfessed sins or soul ties), guard your heart and mind and prepare for warfare. It can happen any time.

Something helpful I learned through a revered prophet and a dear friend of mine was that we can "bind the minds" of hostile non-believers to the mind of Christ. We need to take our seats with Christ in the third Heaven and then exercise our authority to bind the minds of hostile people, to the mind of Christ continuously, until you see the results of their less hostile state. In doing this, you do not interfere with their free will (no one has the authority to do that), but you are simply speaking peace over their mind when you do this.

We also have protection from the evil enemy by the blood of the Lamb. **Revelation 12:11 NKJV** tells us **"And they overcame him by the blood of the Lamb and by the word of their testimony..."** Yeshua shed His Blood for the forgiveness of sins and to purify and redeem us with His Blood. His precious blood is alive and can be applied to us for protection. When the enemy sees the believer or something belonging to the believer that is "covered by the Blood", his attacks cannot prevail against it. All believers who have been cleansed by the Blood also have the right to be protected by it.

What you do is, in prayer and supplication for God, you give Him thanks for the Blood which He shed on the cross for you. Then you ask for the application of the Blood of Yeshua upon yourself, i.e. – your mind, body, will and thoughts, or you can apply it to other people as you are praying for them. You can also apply the Blood during times of warfare over your home or people, limiting the influence and the access of the enemy.

Whenever I used to go to work in a hostile environment, I would do warfare beforehand. I would apply the Blood over the roof and environment of my workplace to keep out any demonic influence or access. I would apply the Blood over the entry and exit points of my office as a safe boundary. Every time I applied the Blood, I would sense a divine safety and comfort because no dark forces were able to intrude. His precious Blood can act as a safe barrier and nothing which is unholy can penetrate. Yeshua's Blood is the purest substance in all of existence, so you can rely on His Blood for ultimate protection.

His Blood also helps us to remain pure in our intentions and will, if we apply it to our mind. It helps us to have the mind of Christ. As we cleanse ourselves thoroughly with the Blood, we tend to walk more in purity and righteousness. His purity rubs on us and if we walk in a purer walk, then we give the enemy less of a foothold in our life and in that sense, protects us. We have to be proactive when walking in the protection of God. If we open doors that are not pure, then we are inviting the enemy to have legal grounds in our lives.

When we realize this, we must confess our sins to the Father and repent. Then we receive forgiveness. When we are in a state of confession, we must always ask for His Blood to cleanse us of all unrighteousness. It is like soap which we use to clean our spiritual state when we dirty it. As we live lives of daily repentance, we need to shower in His Blood daily as well.

"But if we walk in the light as He is in the light, we have fellowship with one another, and the blood of Jesus Christ His Son cleanses us from all sin." – 1 John 1:7 NKJV.

Lean on the Lord constantly for His protection. We must remember to be proactive in this walk by making the effort to keep ourselves protected under His Shadow. We must not forget we have His Armor, which has been fashioned in the Kingdom, at our access and His precious Blood, which provides a safe barrier for us to walk freely from all darkness, in our daily walk with Him.

CHAPTER 7

Salvation Calls

If you want to see His Glory, you must be saved. If you want to have the access to the resources of His Glorious Kingdom, then you must be saved. The Bible teaches us strictly- **"let it be known to you all, and to all the people of Israel, that by the name of Jesus Christ of Nazareth, whom you crucified, whom God raised from the dead, by Him this man stands here before you whole. This is the 'stone which was rejected by you builders, which has become the chief cornerstone.' Nor is there salvation in any other, for there is no other name under heaven given among men by which we must be saved."** – Acts 4: 10-12 NKJV.

Why do you think the enemy has caused so much blasphemy against the name of Jesus Christ in the world we live in today? The enemy will not waste his time going after something that is not in place to save people from certain destruction! The enemy and his demons know and fear the name of Jesus Christ because He is the only One who has trampled the grasp of death and hell. He has overcome all evil. He remains at the top of all creation as the final authority, who has the power to judge and save. Matthew 28:18-20 NKJV "And Jesus came and spoke to them, saying, "All authority has been given to Me in heaven and on earth."

"I am He who lives, and was dead, and behold, I am alive forevermore. Amen. And I have the keys of Hades and of Death." – Revelation 1:18 NKJV. Yeshua sits at the right hand of God with the fullness of power, glory and authority. He holds the keys to hell and has the power to send all demons to hell, including those who have refused the call to salvation.

Hell is a real place. I spoke in an earlier chapter of the horrors of hell and that Yeshua does not send us there, but we choose to go there. Yeshua grieves as each soul is sent to hell because they rejected His free gift of Salvation. He already did all the hard work to get us there and all we have to do is accept His free gift and remain in Him all of our lives.

"For God so loved the world that He gave His only begotten Son, that whoever believes in Him should not perish but have everlasting life. For God did not send His Son into the world to condemn the world, but that the world through Him might be saved." – John 3:16-17 NKJV

The Lord God loved you and continues to love you even in your rebellious state. If you have accepted Him, then He continues to rejoice and love you everyday until the day you are called home to Him. He loved you so very much, that He sent the only solution, to be sacrificed as an offering to God for the sins of all mankind and to do away with the law of sin and death, once and for all! All sinners, no matter what they have done, can receive forgiveness in this life and be cleansed of their sins. When you come into Yeshua's arms, your old sinful identity is done away with, and your new identity of salvation is provided for you. Take the leap of faith and trust Him enough to take you home into His Kingdom, which will never ever end.

"For the wages of sin is death, but the gift of God is eternal life in Christ Jesus our Lord." – Romans 6:23 NKJV

If you remain in the stains and sinful patterns of this world, then you will surely give birth to a great measure of sin which will result in death. Death in this sense is not the physical sense, but the death of your eternal soul, which will be destroyed in hell. Surely, you can agree with me that this world is filled with suffering, pains, death and everything cruel. Look at the news and observe the evil and wicked things which are taking place. This is all the result of the sinful nature of man. Come out of the cycle of sin! Be set free from the world!

The free gift of being saved from this death is found in Yeshua only. He will always pursue you in this life to continuously offer you the free gift of God, but if you choose not to accept it and pass away in rejection of it, there is no second chance when you stand before Him in judgment. Today is the day! This is the best free gift you could ever receive for all eternity.

"Jesus said to him, "I am the way, the truth, and the life. No one comes to the Father except through Me." – John 14:6 NKJV.

Based on who Yeshua was, this is the truth of His message. There is simply no other way to enter in His Kingdom. He is the only way. Allow the Holy Spirit to convict you of this truth as you take the time to meditate on this verse. If you allow Him, He will impress on your heart the great need to follow Him, and only Him. He is the only road to Heaven. He is the truth of all things. He is your newfound born-again life in the Kingdom. If you want to reach God, you have to receive Yeshua.

"But as many as received Him, to them He gave the right to become children of God, to those who believe in His name: who were born,

not of blood, nor of the will of the flesh, nor of the will of man, but of God."

If you receive Yeshua into your heart, He promises you will be born again with a new identity in the Spirit. The fruits and evidence of your new identity will manifest in your life, giving you personal evidence that You have become a new child of the most High God. A son or daughter of God. As a child of God, you become royalty and have the privilege and special access to the secrets of an everlasting Kingdom. You have access to supernatural benefits that is impossible for the world to give you. The Kingdom child status is an identity that you will never have in the world. It lasts forever!

"In Him you also trusted, after you heard the word of truth, the gospel of your salvation; in whom also, having believed, you were sealed with the Holy Spirit of promise, who is the guarantee of our inheritance until the redemption of the purchased possession, to the praise of His glory." – Ephesians 1:13-14 NKJV.

If you become saved after hearing the hopeful message of the Good News of the Gospel, you become sealed with His Holy Spirit. This acts as a Heavenly label or branding so that everything in the supernatural / spirit realm knows that you belong to the King of kings and Lord of lords. He will ensure that your inheritance in heaven, which is greater than any amount of material wealth, is kept safely for you until you walk through the gates of the Kingdom. There you will enjoy eternal glory in the presence of the Father, Son and Holy Spirit.

"That if you confess with your mouth the Lord Jesus and believe in your heart that God has raised Him from the dead, you will be saved." - Romans 10:9 NKJV

Are you willing to receive His salvation now? Please know that the next hour of your life is not promised. Right now, is the best time to make this decision. You need to truly believe that He is the only way and based on your confession in Him, which He eagerly waits for you to make, you can have this free Salvation. My prayer for you is that you will allow the Holy Spirit to convict your heart, so that you may realize you are in need of a savior.

If you are ready, then pray the following:

Lord Jesus Christ of Nazareth,
I believe You are the Son of God and I believe God raised You from the dead. I ask You to come into my life right now as I surrender myself to You wholeheartedly.
Please be Lord of my life and cleanse me of my sins.
Please bring me into Your Kingdom, save me from death and hell, and reveal Yourself to me.
In Jesus Christ's name I thank You for Your salvation. Amen.

Once you have prayed this prayer, immediately look up a local Pentecostal church and attend. Make contact with the pastors and ask them to pray over you. Inform them of this decision you have made and get connected in the church. In this way, you will gain more teaching, understanding and revelation. The Lord promises to never leave you nor forsake you. Bless His name for your newfound freedom and allow Him to work in your life. Let Him lead you everyday.

As a witness to His Glory, I promise, you will not regret this.

I leave you with His Shalom peace and I hope to see you one day in His glorious Kingdom, where I can embrace your personally and remind you how happy we will all be in the Kingdom, that you made this decision.

I love you, my friend. Jesus is Lord.

"It is finished!" – John 19:30 NKJV.

Amen.

ACKNOWLEDGMENTS

I want to Glorify the Lord Jesus Christ, Who sat with me in Spirit to write every page.

I want to thank Helena Kauppinen of Gospel Light Ministries - Upper Room for her insight and prayers for this book: Thank you, revered Apostle and dear friend. I look forward to our time in eternity forever.

I want to also thank Andrea Belmore for helping me to edit this book and continuously providing encouraging insight and commentary, both to this book and my life.

AUTHOR BIO

Keshan Singh has been a Christian since he was 15 years old. He is very grateful that he took the call of God seriously in his life, which led him to write this book. He is very hopeful that the message of Jesus Christ will reach and convict everyone who reads this book, in love.

Keshan lives in Australia and cannot wait to make it to the Father's house.

www.ingramcontent.com/pod-product-compliance
Lightning Source LLC
LaVergne TN
LVHW051605070426
835507LV00021B/2772